# FREEMASONRY EXPOSITION

### EXPOSITION & ILLUSTRATION OF FREEMASONRY
## CAPT. W. M. MORGAN

by
**ONE OF THE FRATERNITY WHO DEVOTED
THIRTY YEARS TO THE SUBJECT**

*"God said let there be light
and there was light"*

*ISBN: 978-1-63923-185-0*

*Printed: March 2022*

*Cover Art By: Amit Paul*

*Published and Distributed By: Lushena Books*
*607 Country Club Drive, Unit E*
*Bensenville, IL 60106*
*www.lushenabooksinc.com/books*

*ISBN: 978-1-63923-185-0*

# INTRODUCTION.

(WRITTEN FOR THE ORIGINAL EDITION.
*By the Publisher, Col. David C. Miller, Batavia, N. Y.*)

In the absence of the author, or rather compiler of the following work, who was kidnapped and carried away from the village of Batavia, on the 11th day of September, 1826, by a number of Freemasons, it devolves upon the publisher to attempt to set forth some of the leading views that governed those who embarked in the undertaking.

To contend with prejudice, and to struggle against customs and opinions, which superstition, time, and ignorance have hallowed, requires time, patience, and magnanimity. When we begin to pull down the strongholds of error, the batteries we level against them, though strong, and powerful; and victorious at last, are at first received with violence; and when in our conquering career we meet with scoffs and revilings from the beseiged partisans of untenable positions, it the more forcibly impresses us we are but men; and that in every work of reformation and renovation we must encounter various difficulties. For a full confirmation of our statement we might refer to the history of the world. It is not our intention, however, to give a full detail of the whims and caprices of man to bring forth the historic records of other years as proof of the windings and shiftings of the various characters who have "Strutted their brief hour on life's stage" in order to convince that customs, associations, and institutions are like the lives of the authors and abettors, fleeting and fragile. Many of them rise up as bubbles on the ocean, and die away. Circumstances give them existence, and when these causes cease to exist, they go into the same gulf of oblivion as countless exploded opinions and tenets have gone before them. The mind that formed and planned them, goes on in its dazzling flight, bounding over barrier after barrier, till it has arrived at the ultimate goal of consummation.

The daily occurrences before us bring forth the full conviction that the emanation from the God of light is gradually ascending to regions of greater intellectual brilliancy.

## IV

When we view man, in the infancy of society, as in the childhood of his existence, he is weak, powerless and defenceless; but in his manhood and riper years, he has grown to his full stature, and stands forth in commanding attitude, the favored and acknowledged lord of the world. For his comfort and well-being as a member of society, rules and regulations are necessary. In the various stages of his progress, these systematic improvements undergo various changes, according to circumstances and situations. What is proper and necessary in one grade of society, is wholly useless, and may be alarming in another. Opinions and usages that go down in tradition, and interfere not with our improvements in social concerns, adhere to us more closely and become entwined in all our feelings. It is to this we owe our bigoted attachment to antiquity—it is this that demands from us a superstitious reverence for the opinions and practices of men of former times, and closes the ear against truth, and blinds the eyes to the glare of new lights and new accessions of knowledge through which medium only can they break in upon the mind.

We have within ourselves the knowledge; and everywhere around us the proofs that we are beings destined not to stand still. In our present state of advancement, we look with pity on the small progress of our fathers in arts and sciences, and social institutions; and when compared with our elevated rank, we have just cause of pride and of grateful feelings. They did well for the times in which they lived, but to the ultimatum of perfectability we are nearer, and in the monuments we have before us of the skill and genius of our times and age, we have only fulfilled these destinies for which we were created; and we object to every obstacle that opposes or attempts to oppose the will of heaven.

In the present enlightened state to which society has advanced, we contend that the opinions and tenets and pretended secrecies of "olden times," handed down to us, should be fully, fairly and freely canvassed; that from the mist and darkness which have hung over them, they should come out before the open light of day, and be subject to the rigid test of candid investigation. These preliminary remarks lead us to the main object of our introduction.

We come to lay before the world the claims of an institution which has been sanctioned by ages, venerated for wis-dom, exalted for "light;" but, an institution whose benefits have always been overrated, and whose continuance is not in the slightest degree, necessary. We meet it with its high requirements, its "time honored customs," its swelling titles, and shall show it in its nakedness and simplicity. Strip it of its "borrowed trappings" and it is a mere nothing, a toy not now worthy the notice of a child to sport with. We look back to it as, at one period, a "cement of society and bond of union"—we view it as, at one time, a venerable fort—but now in ruins—which contained within its walls many things that dignified and adorned human nature. We give it due credit for the services it has done; but at present when light has gone abroad into the utmost recesses and corners of the world—when information is scattered wide around us, and knowledge is not closeted in cloisters and ceils but "stalks abroad with her beams of light, and her honors and rewards," we may now, when our minority has expired, act up to our character and look no longer to Masonry as our guide and conductor; it has nothing in it now valuable that is not known to every inquiring mind. It contains, wrapped up in its supposed mysteries, no useful truth, no necessary knowledge that has not gone forth to the world through other channels and by other means. If we would have a knowledge of sacred history—of the religion and practices of the Jews, and the terms and technicalities of the Mosaic institutions, we can have recourse to the Bible. If we wish further communications from heaven, we have open to our view the pages of the New Testament. If we would "climb the high ascent of human science, and trace the mighty progress of human genius in every gigantic effort of mind in logic, geometry, mathematics, chemistry, and every other branch of knowledge," we ridicule the idea that Masonry, in her retirements, contains the arts and sciences. The sturdiest Mason in the whole fraternity is not bold enough to uphold or maintain the opinion for one moment in sober reality. The origin of the institution is easily traced to the rude ages of the world—to a body of mechanics, or a corporation of oper-ative workmen, who formed signs and regulations, the more easily to carry on their work, and to protect their order. [The very obligations solemnly tendered to every member, carry the strongest internal evidence of the semi-barbarity that prevailed at the time of the institution of the order,] In the course of time, as society increased, and knowledge became more general, it spread, and embracing in its grasp other objects than at first, it enrolled in its ranks men of the first respectability in wealth, talents and worth. But that there is anything intrinsically valuable in the signs, symbols, or words of Masonry, no man of sense will contend. That there is not any hidden secret which operates as a talismanic charm on its possessors, every man of intelligence, Mason or no Mason, must candidly acknowledge. It is worse than idleness for the defenders of the order, at the present day to entrench themselves behind their outward show—the semblance before the world—and to say they are in possession of superior knowledge.

We pretend not to act under a cover. We shall "tell the truth, the whole truth, and nothing but the truth." Masonry, it is true, has long been eulogized in song—it has formed the burthen of the poet's theme, and been the subject of the orator's best performances. Fancy has been almost exhausted in bringing out "new flowers to deck the fairy queen;" but when we come behind the scenes, what is the picture we behold? Are we to rest satisfied with the *ipse dixit* of others, or to examine the truth for ourselves? The touchstone is before our readers in the present publication.

Masonry is of itself naked and worthless. It consists of gleanings from the Holy Scriptures, and from the arts and sciences, which have shone in the world. Linking itself with philosophy and science and religion, on this it rests all its claims to veneration and respect. Take away this borrowed aid, and it falls into ruins.

Much weight is still attached to the argument, that as a tie uniting men—that, as a significant speech, symbolically speaking every language, and at the same time embodying in its constitution everything that is valuable, it should command respect. We meet this argument with facts that cannot be controverted. We put it on a basis that will fling into the back ground every quibble and artifice on the subject; and, in the language of a polemic writer, we challenge opposition to our positon.

The religion inculcated by the Son of Man does all this;

# VII

and in no possible situation can man be placed, that the benign influence of Christianity does not completely supersede the use of a mere human institution. Place a brother in a desert, unfriended and unknown,—leave him in a wilderness where human footsteps never printed the ground, the Divine Benefactor is at his side, and watches over him with parental guidance. Let him be driven on a barbarous coast, in the midst of savage men, and there it is that the breathings of the divine influence spreads around him its shield, brings him into civilized society—in the busy walks of men, and are we to be told, as members of community, sojourners on earth, and candidates for heaven, we must be taught our duty at a Mason's lodge? Wherever Masonry exercises its influence with success, there Christianity can have, or should have a more powerful effect. Whenever Masonry claims "kindred with the skies," and exalts herself above every living sublunary thing, then, with an unhallowed step, it obtrudes on the sacred borders of religion, and decks itself in borrowed garments.

Entrenched within these strong walls—decked with all the glitter of high sounding professions, claiming what does not belong to it,—it dazzles "but to bewilder and destroy." In its train, in these United States, are enrolled many periodical works devoted to Masonry; and under the guise of patronizing mechanics—the arts and sciences—lend their aid to carry on the imposing delusion. They take up the specious title of throwing a little illumination on this benighted country, from their secret depositories. Arrogating to itself what should deck other's brows—assuming to be the parton, the life and soul of all that is great and valuable—it deceives many of its votaries, and from its *gaudy* premises the most untenable and onerous conclusions are drawn.

Are we astonished at the wild and heedless manner in which many of the votaries of Masonry rush into every excess, putting at defiance the laws of our civil institutions, which suffer no one to put in jeopardy, but by due forms, and disregarding the command of the Most High, which says, "Thou shalt not kill?"——we can readily trace the cause to the impressions and practices obtained from its false tenets and descriptive arrogance. Masonry is to the modern world what the whore of Babylon was to the ancient; and is the beast with seven heads and ten horns, ready to tear out our bowels, and *scatter them to the four winds of heaven.*

Masonry gives rogues and evil-minded characters an opportunity of visiting upon their devoted victim, all the ills attending combined power, when exerted to accomplish destruction. It works unseen, at all silent hours, and secret times and places; and, like death when summoning his diseases, pounces upon its devoted subject, and lays him prostrate in the dust. Like the great enemy of man, it has shown its cloven foot, and put the public upon its guard against its secret machinations.

This part of the subject requires no further discussion either by way of ridicule or downright sincerity, but the remark which cannot be too often reiterated, that the world, in its present advanced state, requires no such order for our social intercourse; and when the Masonic mania prevails as it now does in this country, we are exalting a mere human ordinance, with its useless trumpery and laughable accompaniments, for the sublime and unadorned lessons of Heaven.

To some men it is galling and mortifying in the extreme to give up their darling systems. With the increase of years their fondness becomes so great that they cling to them with wild and bewildered attachment. But we would ask them, where now are the Knights of Malta and Jerusalem, and the objects that called forth their perils and journeyings? Where are the crusades and excursions on which our Grand Commanders, Generalissimos and Sir Knights are to be engaged. . . . . . . . In no other excursions than Cervantes describes of his redoubtable hero *Don Quixote.* The days and occasions that called forth these deeds of chivalry and valor have passed like those before the flood; and the *mock* dignitaries and *puppet show* actions of Masons in their imitation call forth pity and indignation. When we now see the gaudy show in a lodge-room, and a train of nominal officers with their distinction and badges, it may give us some faint idea of scenes that are past, and may gratify an idle curiosity, but produces no substantial good under heaven. When monasteries and cloisters, and inquisitor's cells and prisons have been broken up before the sweeping march of the moral mind, why this unnecessary mummery should be so much countenanced in this country, above all other countries in the world, is a matter of astonishment.

The day we trust will never arrive here, when ranks in Masonry will be stepping-stones to places of dignity and power—when this institution will be a machine to press down the free born spirit of men. We have now no tyrant to rule over us—no kingly potentate to move over our heads the rod of authority; but high in our elevation, and invincible in our strongholds, we put at defiance secret cabals and associations. The public opinion is like a mighty river, and gigantic in its course it will sweep every interposing obstacle before it.

In the work which we submit to the public we have given false coloring to nothing; nor in these remarks have we set down aught in malice. In the firm discharge of our undertaking we have been stern and unbending as the rugged mountain oak; and persecutions, pains and perils have not deterred us from our purpose. We have triumphed over tumult, and clamor, and evil speaking.

When our book goes out to the world, it will meet with attacks of a violent nature from one source, and men of mock titles and order will endeavor to heap upon it every calumny. Men more tenacious of absolute forms and practice than they are attentive to truth and honor, will deny our expositions, and call us liars and impostors.

Such is the treatment, however ungenerous and unjust, which we expect to meet, and for which we are prepared. Truth, we know, is majestic and will finally prevail. The little petty effusions of malice that will be thrown out, will die with their authors, whom this work will survive.

We now aver, in defiance of whatever may be said to the contrary—no matter by whom, how exalted his rank—that this book is what it pretends to be; that it is a master key to the secrets of Masonry; that in the pages before him. the man of candor and inquiry can judge for himself, and then a proper judgment will be formed of our intention.

# ILLUSTRATIONS
## —OF—
# MASONRY, ETC.

A. Description of the Ceremonies used in opening a
Lodge of Entered Apprentice Masons; which is the
same in all upper degrees, with the exception
of the difference in the signs, due-guards,
grips, pass-grips, words and their several names; all of which will be
given and explained in their
proper places as the
work progresses.

One rap calls the lodge to order—one calls up the Junior
and Senior Deacons—two raps call up all the subordinate
officers, and three, all the members of the lodge.

The Master having called the lodge to order, and the officers
all seated, the Master says to the Junior Warden, 'Brother
Junior, are they all Entered Apprentice Masons in the south?'

Ans. 'They are, Worshipful.'

Master to the Senior Warden, 'Brother Senior, are they all
Entered Apprentice Masons in the west?'

Ans. 'They are, Worshipful.'

The Master then says, 'They are, in the east,' at the same
time he gives a rap with the common gavel or mallet, which
calls up both Deacons.

Master to Junior Deacon, 'Brother Junior, the first care of
a Mason?'

Ans. 'To see the lodge tyled, Worshipful.'

Master to Junior Deacon, 'Attend to that part of your duty,
and inform the Tyler that we are about to open a lodge of
Entered Apprentice Masons, and direct him to tyle accordingly.' The Junior Deacon then steps to the door and gives
three raps, which are answered by three raps from without;
the Junior Deacon then gives one, which is also answered by
the Tyler with one; the door is then partly opened and the
Junior Deacon delivers his message, and resumes his situation

**and** says, 'The door is tyled, Worshipful.' (at the same time giving the due-guard, which is never omitted when the Master **is** addressed.)

The Master to Junior Deacon, 'Brother, by whom?'

Ans. 'By a Master Mason without the door, armed with the proper implement of his office.'

Master to Junior Deacon, 'His duty there?'

Ans. 'To keep off all cowans and eaves-droppers, see that none pass or repass without permission from the Master.' (Some say without permission from the chair.)

Master to Junior Deacon, 'Brother Junior, your place in the lodge?'

Ans. 'At the right hand of the Senior Warden in the west.'

Master to Junior Deacon, 'Your business there, Brother Junior?'

Ans. 'To wait on the Worshipful Master and Wardens, act as their proxy in the active duties of the lodge, and take charge of the door.'

Master to Junior Deacon, 'The Senior Deacon's place in the lodge?'

Ans. 'At the right hand of the Worshipful Master in the east.' [The Master, while asking the last questions gives two raps, which call up all the subordinate officers.]

Master to Senior Deacon, 'Your duty there, Brother Senior?'

Ans. 'To wait on the Worshipful Master and Wardens, act as their proxy in the active duties of the lodge, attend to the preparation and introduction of candidates, and welcome and clothe all visiting Brethren. [*i. e.,* furnish them with an apron.]

Master to Senior Deacon, 'The Secretary's place in the lodge, Brother Senior?'

Ans. 'At the left hand of the Worshipful Master in the east.'

Master to the Secretary, 'Your duty there, Brother Secretary?'

Ans. 'The better to observe the Worshipful Master's will and pleasure, record the proceedings of the lodge; transmit a copy of the same to the Grand Lodge, if required; receive all moneys and money bills from the hands of the Brethren, pay them over to the Treasurer, and take his receipt for the same.'

The Master to the Secretary, 'The Treasurer's place in the lodge?'

Ans. 'At the right hand of the Worshipful Master.'

Master to Treasurer, 'Your duty there, Brother Treasurer?'

Ans. 'Duly to observe the Worshipful Master's will and pleasure; receive all moneys and money bills from the hands of the Secretary; keep a just and true account of the same; pay them out by order of the Worshipful Master and consent of the Brethren.'

The Master to the Treasurer, "The Junior Warden's place in the lodge, Brother Treasurer?'

Ans. 'In the south, Worshipful.'

Master to Junior Warden, 'Your business there, Brother Junior?'

Ans. 'As the sun in the south at high meridian is the beauty and glory of the day, so stands the Junior Warden in the south, the better to observe the time, call the crafts from labor to refreshment, superintend them during the hours thereof, see that none convert the hours of refreshment into that of intemperance or excess; and call them out again in due season, that the Worshipful Master may have honor, and they profit and pleasure thereby.'

Master to the Junior Warden, 'The Senior Warden's place in the lodge?'

Ans. 'In the west, Worshipful.'

Master to Senior Warden, 'Your duty there, Brother Senior?'

Ans. 'As the sun sets in the west to close the day, so stands the Senior Warden in the west to assist the Worshipful Master in opening his lodge, take care of the jewels and implements, see that none be lost, pay the craft their wages, if any be due, and see that none go away dissatisfied.'

Master to the Senior Warden, 'The Master's place in the lodge?'

Ans. 'In the east, Worshipful.'

Master to the Senior Warden, 'His duty there?'

Ans. 'As the sun rises in the east to open and adorn the

# Lodge of Entered Apprentices,

## FELLOW CRAFTS,

—OR—

# MASTER MASONS.

Treasurer.    Worshipful Master.    Secretary.

Senior Deacon.

Altar.    Junior Warden.

Senior Warden.    Junior Deacon.

day, so presides the Worshipful Master in the east to open and adorn his lodge, set his crafts to work with good and wholesome laws, or cause the same to be done.' The Master now gives three raps, when all the brethren rise, and the Master taking off his hat, proceeds as follows : In like manner so do I, strictly forbidding all profane language, private committees, or any other disorderly conduct whereby the peace and narmony of this lodge may be interrupted while engaged in its lawful pursuits, under no less penalty than the by-laws, or such penalty as the majority of the Brethren present may see fit to inflict. Brethren, attend to giving the signs.' [Here lodges differ very much. In some they declare the lodge opened as follows, before they give the signs :]

Due-Guard.Entered Apprentice.   Penal Sign.

The Master (all the Brethren imitating him) extends his left arm from his body so as to form an angle of about forty-five degrees, and holds his right hand transversely across his left, the palms thereof about one inch apart. This is called the Due Guard, and alludes to the position a Candidate's hands are placed in when he takes the obligation of an Entered Apprentice Mason. The Master then draws his right hand across his throat, the hand open, with the thumb next to his throat, and drops it down by his side. This is called the penal sign of an Entered Apprentice Mason, (many call it sign) and alludes to the penalty of the obligation. (See obligation.) The Master then declares the lodge opened in the following manner: 'I now declare this lodge of Entered Apprentice Masons duly opened for dispatch of business.' The Senior Warden declares it to the Junior Warden, and he to the Brethren. 'Come, Brethren, let us pray.'—One of the following prayers is used:

Most holy and glorious God! the great architect of the Universe; the giver of all good gifts and graces: Thou hast promised that 'Where two or three are gathered together in thy name, thou wilt be in the midst of them and bless them.' In thy name we assemble, most humbly beseeching thee to bless us in all our undertakings; that we may know and serve thee aright, and that all our actions may tend to thy glory and our advancement in knowledge and virtue. And we beseech thee, O Lord God, to bless our present assembling; and to illuminate our minds through the influence of the Son of Righteousness, that we may walk in the light of thy countenance; and when the trials of our probationary state are over, be admitted into the temple, not made with hands, eternal in the heavens. Amen. So mote it be.

*Another prayer, as often used at opening as closing*:

Behold, how good and pleasant it is for brethren to dwell together in unity; it is like the precious ointment upon the head, that ran down upon the beard, even Aaron's beard, that went down to the skirts of his garment; as the dew of Hermon, and as the dew that descended upon the mountains of Zion, for there the Lord commanded the blessing, even life forever more. Amen. So mote it be.

The lodge being now open and ready to proceed to business, the Master directs the Secretary to read the minutes of the last meeting, which naturally brings to view the business of the present.

If there are any candidates to be brought forward, that will be the first business to be attended to. I will therefore proceed with a description of the ceremonies used in the admission and initiation of a candidate into the first degree of Masonry.

A person wishing to become a Mason must get some one who is a Mason to present his petition to a lodge, when, if there are no serious objections, it will be entered on the minutes, and a committee of two or three appointed to enquire into his character, and report to the next regular communication. The following is a form of petition used by a candidate; but a worthy candidate will not be rejected for the want of formality in his petition:

To the Worshipful Master, Wardens and Brethren of Lodge No. —, of Free and Accepted Masons.

The subscriber, residing in ———, of lawful age, and by occupation a ————, begs leave to state that, unbiased by friends, and uninfluenced by mercenary motives, he freely and voluntarily offers himself a candidate for the mysteries of Masonry, and that he is prompted to solicit this privilege by a favorable opinion conceived of the institution. a desire of knowledge, and a sincere wish of being serviceable tc his fellow creatures. Should his petition be granted, he will cheerfully conform to all the ancient established usages and customs of the fraternity.

(Signed)         A. B.

At the next regular communication, (if no very serious objection appears against the candidate) the ballot boxes will be passed; one black ball will reject a candidate. The boxes may be passed three times. The Deacons are the proper persons to pass them. One of the boxes has black and white beans or balls in it, the other empty, the one with the balls in it goes before, and furnishes each member with a black and white ball; the empty box follows and receives them. There are two holes in the top of this box with a small tube, (generally) in each, one of which is black and the other white, with a partition in the box. The members put both their balls into this box as their feelings dictate; when the balls are received, the box is presented to the Master, Senior and Junior Wardens, who pronounce clear or not clear, as the case may be. The ballot proving clear, the candidate (if present) is conducted into a small preparation room, adjoining the lodge when he is asked the following questions and gives the following answers. Senior Deacon to Candidate, "Do you sincerely declare, upon your honor before these gentlemen, that, unbiased by friends, uninfluenced by unworthy motives, you freely and voluntarily offer yourself a candidate for the mysteries of Masonry.?"

Ans. "I do."

Senior Deacon to candidate. "Do you sincerely declare, upon your honor before these gentlemen, that you are prompted to solicit the privileges of Masonry by a favorable opinion conceived of the institution, a desire of knowledge, and a sincere wish of being serviceable to your fellow creatures?"

Ans. "I do."

Senior Deacon to candidate, "Do you sincerely declare upon your honor before these gentlemen, that you will cheerfully conform to all the ancient established usages and customs of the fraternity?"

Ans. "I do."

After the above questions are proposed and answered and the result reported to the Master, he says, "Brethren at the request of Mr. A. B. he has been proposed and accepted in regular form. I therefore recommend him as a proper candidate for the mysteries of Masonry and worthy to partake of the privileges of the fraternity and in consequence of a declaration of his intentions, voluntarily made, I believe he will cheerfully conform to the rules of the order."

The candidate during the time is divested of all his apparel (shirt excepted) and furnished with a pair of drawers kept in the lodge for the use of candidates. The candidate is then blindfolded, his left foot bare, his right in a slipper, his left breast and arm naked, and a rope called a Cable-tow round his neck and left arm, [the rope is not put round the arm in all lodges] in which posture the candidate is conducted to the door where he is caused to give, or the conductor gives three distinct knocks, which are answered by three from within; the conductor gives one more, which is also answered by one from within. The door is then partly opened and the Senior Deacon generally asks, 'Who comes there? Who comes there? Who comes there?"

The conductor, alias the Junior Deacon answers, "A poor blind candidate who has long been desirous of having and receiving a part of the rights and benefits of this worshipful lodge, dedicated (some say erected) to God, and held forth to the holy order of St. John, as all true fellows and brothers have done who have gone this way before him."

The Senior Deacon then asks, "Is it of his own free will and accord he makes this request? Is he duly and truly prepared? worthy and well qualified? and properly avouched for?" All of which being answered in the affirmative, the Senior Deacon to the Junior Deacon: "By what further rights does he expect to obtain this benefit?"

Ans. "By being a man, free born, of lawful age. and under the tongue of good report."

The Senior Deacon then says, "Since this is the case, you will wait till the Worshipful Master in the east is made acquainted with his request, and his answer returned." The Senior Deacon repairs to the Master, when the same questions are asked and answers returned as at the door; after which the Master says, "Since he comes endowed with all these necessary qualifications, let him enter this worshipful lodge in the name of the Lord, and take heed on what he enters." The candidate then enters, the Senior Deacon at the same time pressing his naked left breast with the point of the compass, and asks the candidate, "Did you feel anything?"

Ans. "I did."

Senior Deacon to candidate, "What was it?"

Ans. "A torture."

The Senior Deacon then says, "As this is a torture to your flesh, so may it ever be to your mind and conscience if ever you should attempt to reveal the secrets of Masonry unlawfully." The candidate is then conducted to the centre of the lodge, where he and the Senior Deacon kneel, and the Deacon says the following prayer:

"Vouchsafe thine aid, Almighty Father of the universe, to this our present convention; and grant that this candidate for Masonry may dedicate and devote his life to thy service, and become a true and faithful brother among us. Endue him with a competency of thy divine wisdom, that by the secrets of our art he may be the better enabled to display the beauties of holiness, to the honor of thy holy name." So mote it be—Amen!"

The Master then asks the candidate, "In whom do you put your trust?"

Ans. "In God."

The Master then takes him by the right hand and says, "Since in God you put your trust, arise, follow your leader and fear no danger." The Senior Deacon then conducts the candidate three times regularly round the lodge, and halts at the Junior Warden in the south, where the same questions are asked and answers returned as at the door.

As the candidate and conductor are passing round the room, the Master reads the following passage of Scripture, and takes the same time to read it that they do to go round the lodge three times.

"Behold how good and how pleasant it is for brethren to dwell together in unity! It is like the precious ointment upon the head, that ran down upon the beard, even Aaron's beard, that went down to the skirts of his garment as the dew of Hermon, and as the dew that descended upon the mountains of Zion, for there the Lord commanded the blessing, even life for evermore."

The candidate is then conducted to the Senior Warden in the west, where the same questions are asked and answers returned as before, from whence he is conducted to the Worshipful Master in the east, where the same questions are asked and answers returned as before. The Master likewise demands of him from whence he came and whither he is traveling.

The candidate answers, "from the west and traveling to the east."

Master inquires, "Why do you leave the west and travel to the east?"

Ans. "In search of light."

Master then says, "Since the candidate is traveling in search of light, you will please conduct him back to the west, from whence he came, and put him in the care of the Senior Warden, who will teach him how to approach the east, the place of light, by advancing upon one upright regular step, to the first step, his feet forming the right angle of an oblong square, his body erect at the altar, before the Master, and place him in a proper position to take upon him the solemn oath or obligation of an Entered Apprentice Mason." The Senior Warden receives the candidate, and instructs him as directed. He first steps off with the left foot and brings up the heel of the right into the hollow thereof; the heel of the right foot against the ankle of the left, will of course form the right angle of an oblong square; the candidate then kneels on his left knee, and places his right foot so as to form a square with the left; he turns his foot round until the ankle bone is as much in front of him as the toes on the left foot, the

candidate's left hand is then put under the Holy Bible, square and compass, and the right on them. This is the position in which a candidate is placed when he takes upon him the oath or obligation of an Entered Apprentice Mason. As soon as the candidate is placed in this position, the Worshipful Master approaches him, and says, "Mr. A. B., you are now placed in a proper position to take upon you the solemn oath or obligation of an Entered Apprentice Mason, which I assure you is neither to affect your religion or politics. If you are willing to take it, repeat your name and say after me:" [And although many have refused to take any kind of an obligation, and begged for the privilege of retiring, yet none have ever made their escape; they have been either coerced or persuaded to submit. There are thousands who never return to the lodge after they are initiated.] The following obligation is then administered:

I, A. B., of my own free will and accord, in presence of Almighty God and this worshipful lodge of Free and Accepted Masons, dedicated to God, and held forth to the holy order of St. John, do hereby and hereon most solemnly and sincerely promise and swear that I will always hail, ever conceal and never reveal any part or parts, art or arts, point or points of the secret arts and mysteries of ancient Freemasonry which I have received, am about to receive, or may hereafter be instructed in, to any person or persons in the known world, except it be to a true and lawful brother Mason, or within the body of a just and lawfully constituted lodge of such; and not unto him, nor unto them whom I shall hear so to be, but unto him and them only whom I shall find so to be after strict trial and due examination, or lawful information. Furthermore, do I promise and swear that I will not write, print, stamp, stain, hew, cut, carve, indent, paint, or engrave it on any thing movable or immovable, under the whole canopy of heaven, whereby or whereon the least letter, figure, character, mark, stain, shadow, or resemblance of the same may become legible or intelligible to myself or any other person in the known world, whereby the secrets of Masonry may be unlawfully obtained through my unworthiness. To all of which I do most solemnly and sincerely promise and swear, without the least equivocation, mental reservation, or self evasion of mind in me whatever; binding myself under no less penalty than to have my throat cut across, my tongue torn out by the roots, and my body buried in the rough sands of the sea at low water-mark, where the tide ebbs and flows twice in twenty-four hours; so help me God, and keep me steadfast in the due performance of the same."

After the obligation the Master addresses the candidate in the following manner: "Brother, to you the secrets of Masonry are about to be unveiled, and a brighter sun never shone lustre on your eyes; while prostrate before this sacred altar, do you not shudder at every crime? Have you not confidence in every virtue? May these thoughts ever inspire you with the most noble sentiments; may you ever feel that elevation of soul that shall scorn a dishonest act. Brother, what do you most desire?"

Ans. "Light."

Master to brethren, "Brethren, stretch forth your hands and assist in bringing this new made brother from darkness to light." The members having formed a circle round the candidate, the Master says, "And God said let there be light, and there was light." At the same time all the brethren clap their hands, and stamp on the floor with their right foot as heavy as possible, the bandage dropping from the candidate's eyes at the same instant, which, after having been so long blind, and full of fearful apprehensions all the time, this great and sudden transition from perfect darkness to a brighter [if possible] than the meridian sun in a mid-summer day, sometimes produces an alarming effect. I once knew a man to faint on being brought to light; and his recovery was quite doubtful for some time; however, he did come to, but he never returned to the lodge again. I have often conversed with him on the subject; he is yet living, and will give a certificate in support of the above statement at any time if requested.

After the candidate is brought to light, the Master addresses him as follows: "Brother, on being brought to light, you first discover three great lights in Masonry, by the assistance of three lesser; they are thus explained: the three great lights in Masonry are the Holy Bible, Square and Compass. The Holy Bible is given to us as a rule and guide for our faith and practice; the Square, to square our actions, and the Compass to keep us in due bounds with all mankind, but more especially with the brethren. The three lesser lights are three burning tapers, or candles placed on candlesticks (some say, or candles on pedestals) they represent the sun, moon, and Master of the lodge, and are thus explained. As the sun rules the day and the moon governs the night, so ought the worshipful Master with equal regularity to rule and govern his lodge, or cause the same to be done; you next discover me, as Master of this lodge, approaching you from the east upon the first step of Masonry, under the sign and due-guard of an Entered Apprentice Mason. (The sign and due-guard has been explained.) This is the manner of giving them; imitate me as near as you can, keeping your position. First step off with your left foot, and bring the heel of the right into the hollow thereof, so as to form a square. [This is the first step in Masonry.] The following is the sign of an Entered Apprentice Mason, and is the sign of distress in this degree; you are not to give it unless in distress. [It is given by holding your two hands transversely across each other, the right hand upwards and one inch from the left.] The following is the due-guard of an Entered Apprentice Mason. [This is given by drawing your right hand across your throat, the thumb next to your throat, your arm as high as the elbow in a horizontal position.] "Brother, I now present you my right hand in token of brotherly love and esteem, and with it the grip and name of the grip of an Entered Apprentice

Mason." The rights hands are joined together as in shaking hands and each sticks his thumb nail into the third joint or upper end of the forefinger; the name of the grip is *Boaz,* and is to be given in the following manner and no other; the Master first gives the grip and word, and divides it for the instruction of the candidate; the questions are as follows: The Master and candidate holding each other by the grip, as before described, the Master says, "What is this?"

Ans. "A grip."

"A grip of what?"

Ans. "The grip of an Entered Apprentice Mason."

"Has it a name?"

Ans. "It has."

"Will you give it to me?"

Ans. "I did not so receive it, neither can I so impart it."

"What will you do with it?"

Ans. "Letter it or halve it."

"Halve it and begin."

Ans. "You begin."

"Begin you."

Ans. "B-O."

"A-Z."

Ans. "BOAZ."

Master says, "Right, brother Boaz, I greet you. It is the name of the left hand pillar of the porch of King Solomon's temple. Arise, brother Boaz, and salute the Junior and Senior Wardens, as such, and convince them that you have been regularly initiated as an Entered Apprentice Mason, and have got the sign, grip and word." The Master returns to his seat while the Wardens are examining the candidate, and gets a lambskin or white apron, presents it to the candidate, and observes, "Brother, I now present you with a lambskin or white apron. It is an emblem of innocence, and the badge of a Mason—it has been worn by kings, princes and potentates of the earth, who have never been ashamed to wear it. It is more honorable than the diadems of kings, or pearls of princesses, when worthily worn; it is more ancient than the Golden Fleece or Roman Eagle, more honorable than the Star and Garter, or any other order that can be conferred upon you at this or any other time, except it be in the body of a just and lawfully constituted lodge; you will carry it to the Senior Warden in the west, who will teach you how to wear it as an Entered Apprentice Mason." The Senior Warden ties the apron on, and turns up the flap instead of letting it fall down in front of the top of the apron. This is the way Entered Apprentice Masons wear, or ought to wear their aprons until they are advanced. The candidate is now conducted to the Master in the east, who says, "Brother, as you are dressed, it is necessary you should have tools to work with; I will now present you with the working tools of an Entered Apprentice

Mason, which are the twenty-four inch gauge and common gavel; they are thus explained:—The twenty-four inch gauge is an instrument made use of by operative Masons to measure and lay out their work, but we as Free and Accepted Masons make use of it for the more noble and glorious purpose of dividing our time. The twenty-four inches on the gauge are emblematical of the twenty-four hours in the day, which we are taught to divide into three equal parts, whereby we find eight hours for the service of God, and a worthy, distressed brother, eight hours for our usual vocations, and eight for refreshment and sleep; the common gavel is an instrument made use of by operative Masons to break off the corners of rough stones, the better to fit them for the builder's use, but we, as Free and Accepted Masons, use it for the more noble and glorious purpose of divesting our hearts and consciences of all the vices and superfluities of life, thereby fitting our minds as living and lively stones, for that spiritual building, that house not made with hands, eternal in the heavens. I also present you with a new name; it is CAUTION; it teaches you that as you are barely instructed in the rudiments of Masonry, that you should be cautious over all your words and actions, particularly when before the enemies of Masonry. I shall next present you with three precious jewels, which are a listening ear, a silent tongue, and a faithful heart. A listening ear teaches you to listen to the instructions of the Worshipful Master; but more especially that you should listen to the calls and cries of a worthy, distressed brother. A silent tongue teaches you to be silent while in the lodge that the peace and harmony thereof may not be disturbed, but more especially that you should be silent before the enemies of Masonry that the craft may not be brought into disrepute by your imprudence. A faithful heart teaches you to be faithful to the instructions of the Worshipful Master at all times, but more especially, that you should be faithful, and keep and conceal the secrets of Masonry, and those of a brother, when given to you in charge, as such; that they may remain as secure and inviolable in your breast as in his own, before communicated to you. I further present you with checkwords, two; their names are *truth* and *union,* and are thus explained: Truth is a divine attribute and the foundation of every virtue; to be good and true, is the first lesson we are taught in Masonry; on this theme we contemplate, and by its dictates endeavor to regulate our conduct; hence, while influenced by this principle, hypocrisy and deceit are unknown among us; sincerity and plain dealing distinguish us, and the heart and tongue join in promoting each other's welfare and rejoicing in each other's prosperity.

Union is that kind of friendship which ought to appear conspicuous in every Mason's conduct. It is so closely allied to the divine attribute, truth, that he who enjoys the one, is seldom destitute of the other. Should interest, honor, prejudice, or human depravity ever induce you to violate any part of the sacred trust we now repose in you, let these two important words, at the earliest insinuation, teach you to pull on the check-line of truth, which will infallibly direct you to pursue that straight and narrow path which ends in the full enjoyment of the Grand Lodge above, where we shall all meet as Masons and members of the same family, in peace, harmony, and love; where all discord on account of politics, religion, or private opinion shall be unknown and banished from within your walls.

Brother, it has been a custom from time immemorial to demand, or ask from a newly made brother, something of a metallic kind, not so much on account of its intrinsic value, but that it may be deposited in the archives of the lodge, as a memorial, that you were herein made a Mason;—a small trifle will be sufficient,—anything of a metallic kind will do; if you have no money, anything of a metallic nature will be sufficient: even a button will do." [The candidate says he has nothing about him; it is known he has nothing.] "Search yourself," the Master replies. He is assisted in searching, nothing is found. "Perhaps you can borrow a trifle," says the Master. [He tries to borrow, none will lend him—he proposes to go into the other room where his clothes are; he is not permitted. If a stranger, he is very embarrassed.] Master to candidate, "Brother, let this ever be a striking lesson to you and teach you, if you should ever see a friend, or more especially a brother in a like penniless situation, to contribute as liberally to his relief as his situation may require, and your abilities will admit, without material injury to yourself or family." Master to Senior Deacon.

"You will conduct the candidate back from whence he came, and invest him of what he has been divested, and let him return for further instruction." The candidate is then conducted to the preparation room, and invested of what he had been divested, and returns to the north-east corner of the lodge, and is taught how to stand upright like a man; when and where the following charge is, or ought to be delivered to him; though it is omitted nine times out of ten, as are near one-half of the ceremonies.

Master to candidate, "Brother, as you are now initiated into the first principles of Masonry, I congratulate you on having been accepted into this ancient and honorable order; ancient, as having subsisted from time immemorial; and honorable, as tending in every particular so to render all men who will become conformable to its principles. No institution was ever raised on a better principle, or more solid foundation, nor were ever more excellent rules and useful maxims laid down than are inculcated in the several Masonic lectures. The greatest and best of men in all ages have been encouragers and promoters of the art, and have never deemed it derogatory to their dignity to level themselves with the fraternity, extend their privileges, and patronize their assemblies."

There are three great duties, which, as a Mason, you are charged to inculcate. To God, your neighbor, and yourself. To God, in never mentioning his name but with that reverential awe that is due from a creature to his Creator; to implore his aid in all your laudable undertakings, and to esteem him as the chief good—To your neighbor, in acting upon the square and doing unto him as you wish he should do unto you; and to yourself in avoiding all irregularity, or intemperance which may impair your faculties, or debase the dignity of your profession. A zealous attachment to these principles will ensure public and private esteem. In the state you are to be a quiet and peaceable subject, true to your government and just to your country; you are not to countenance disloyalty, but faithfully submit to legal authority, and conform with cheerfulness to the government of the country in which you live. In your outward demeanor be particularly careful to avoid censure or reproach. Although your frequent appearance at our regular meetings is earnestly solicited, yet it is not meant that Masonry should interfere with your necessary vocations; for these are on no account to be neglected; neither are you to suffer your zeal for the institution to lead you into argument with those, who, through ignorance, may ridicule it. At your leisure hours, that you may improve in Masonic knowledge, you are to converse with well-informed brethren, who will be always as ready to give, as you will be to receive information. Finally, keep sacred and inviolable the mysteries of the order, as these are to distinguish you from the rest of the community, and mark your consequence among Masons. If, in the circle of your acquaintance, you find a person desirous of being initiated into Masonry, be particularly attentive not to recommend him, unless you are convinced he will conform to our rules, that the honor, glory, and reputation of the institution may be firmly established, and the world at large convinced of its good effects."

The work of the evening being over, I will proceed to give a description of the manner of closing the lodge. It is a very common practice in lodges to close a lodge of Entered Apprentices, and open a lodge of Fellow Crafts, and close that, and open a Master Mason's lodge, all in the same evening.

Some brother generally makes a motion that the lodge be closed; it being seconded and carried:—

The Master to the Junior Deacon—"Brother Junior," [giving one rap which calls up both Deacons,] "the first as well as the last care of a Mason?

Ans. "To see the lodge tyled, Worshipful."

Master to Junior Deacon, "Attend to that part of your duty, and inform the Tyler that we are about to close this lodge of Entered Apprentice Masons, and direct him to tyle accordingly." The Junior Deacon steps to the door and gives three raps, which are answered by the Tyler with three more; the Junior Deacon then gives one, which is also answered by the Tyler by one. The Junior Deacon then opens the door, delivers his message, and resumes his place in the lodge and says, "The door is tyled, Worshipful."

Master to Junior Deacon, "By whom?"

Ans. "By a Master Mason without the door, armed with the proper implements of his office."

Master to Junior Deacon, "His business there?"

Ans. "To keep off all cowans and eavesdroppers and see that none pass or repass without permission from the chair."

Master to Junior Deacon, "Your place in the lodge, brother Junior?"

Ans. "At the right hand of the Senior Warden in the west."

Master to Junior Deacon, "Your duty there?"

Ans. "To wait on the Worshipful. Master and Wardens, act as their proxy in the active duties of the lodge, and take charge of the door."

Master to the Junior Deacon, "The Senior Deacon's place in the lodge?"

Ans. "At the right hand of the Worshipful Master in the east."

Master to Senior Deacon, "Your duty there, brother Senior?"

Ans. "To wait on the Worshipful Master and Wardens, act as their proxy in the active duties of the lodge, attend to the preparation and introduction of candidates, receive and clothe all visiting brethren."

Master to the Senior Deacon, "The Secretary's place in the lodge?"

Ans. "At your left hand, Worshipful."

Master to Secretary, "Your duty there, brother Secretary?"

Ans. "Duly to observe the Master's will and pleasure; record the proceedings of the lodge; transmit a copy of the same to the Grand Lodge, if required; receive all moneys and money bills from the hands of the brethren; pay them over to the Treasurer, and take his receipt for the same."

Master to the Secretary, "The Treasurer's place in the lodge?"

Ans. "At the right hand of the Worshipful Master."

Master to Treasurer, "Your business there, brother Treasurer?"

Ans. "Duly to observe the Worshipful Master's will and pleasure; receive all moneys and money bills from the hands of the Secretary; keep a just and accurate account of the same; pay them out by order of the Worshipful Master and consent of the brethren."

Master to the Treasurer, "The Junior Warden's place in the lodge?"

Ans. "In the south, Worshipful."

Master to the Junior Warden, "Your business there, brother Junior?"

Ans. "As the sun in the south, at high meridian, is the beauty and glory of the day, so stands the Junior Warden in the south, at high twelve, the better to observe the time; call the crafts from labor to refreshment; superintend them during the hours thereof; see that none convert the purposes of refreshment into that of excess or intemperance; call them on again in due season, that the Worshipful Master may have honor, and they pleasure and profit thereby."

The Master to the Junior Warden, [I wish the reader to take particular notice that in closing the lodge the Master asks the Junior Warden as follows: "The Master's place in the lodge?" and in opening he asks the Senior Warden the same question.] "The Master's place in the lodge?"

Ans. "In the east, Worshipful."

Master to Junior Warden, "His duty there?"

Ans. "As the sun rises in the east to open and adorn the day, so presides the Worshipful Master in the east to open and adorn his lodge; set his crafts to work with good and wholesome laws, or cause the same to be done."

Master to Junior Warden, "The Senior Warden's place in the lodge?"

Ans. "In the west, Worshipful."

Master to Senior Warden, "Your business there, brother Senior?"

Ans. "As the sun sets in the west to close the day, so stands the Senior Warden in the west to assist the Worshipful Master in opening and closing the lodge; take care of the jewels and implements; see that none be lost; pay the crafts their wages, if any be due, and see that none go away dissatisfied."

The Master now gives three raps, when all the brethren rise, and the Master asks, "Are you all satisfied?" They answer in the affirmative, by giving the due-guard. Should the Master discover that any declined giving it, inquiry is immediately made why it is so; and if any member is dissatisfied with any part of the proceedings, or with any brother, the subject is immediately investigated. Master to the brethren, "Attend to giving the signs; as I do so do you; give them downwards" (which is by giving the last in opening, first in closing. In closing, on this degree, you first draw your right hand across your throat, as herein before described, and then hold your two hands over each other as before described. This is the method pursued through all the degrees; and when opening on any of the upper degrees, all their signs, of all the preceding degrees, are given before you give the signs of the degree on which you are opening.) This being done, the Master proceeds, "I now declare this lodge of Entered Apprentice Masons regularly closed in due and ancient form. Brother Junior Warden, please inform brother Senior Warden, and request him to inform the brethren that it is my will and pleasure that this lodge of Entered Apprentice Masons be now closed, and stand closed until our next regular communication, unless a case or cases of emergency shall require earlier convention, of which every member shall be notified; during which time it is seriously hoped and expected that every brother will demean himself as becomes a Free and Accepted Mason." Junior Warden to Senior Warden, "Brother Senior, it is the Worshipful Master's will and pleasure that this lodge of Entered Apprentice Masons be closed, and stand closed until our next regular communication, unless a case or cases of emergency shall require earlier convention, of which every brother shall be notified; during which time it is seriously hoped and expected that every brother will demean himself as becomes a Free and Accepted Mason." Senior Warden to the brethren, "Brethren, you have heard the Worshipful Master's will and pleasure, as communicated to me by brother Junior; so let it be done." Master to the Junior Warden, "Brother Junior, how do Masons meet?"

Ans. 'On the level."

Master to Senior Warden, "How do Masons part?"

Ans. "On the square."

Master to the Junior and Senior Wardens, "Since we meet on the level, brother Junior, and part on the square, brother Senior, so let us ever meet and part, in the name of the Lord." Here follows a prayer sometimes used. Master to the brethren, "Brethren, let us pray."

"Supreme Architect of the Universe! accept our humble praises for the many mercies and blessings which thy bounty has conferred upon us, and especially for this friendly and social intercourse. Pardon, we beseech thee, whatever thou hast seen amiss in us since we have been together; and continue to us thy presence, protection and blessing. Make us sensible of the renewed obligations we are under to love thee supremely, and to be friendly to each other. May all our irregular passions be subdued; and may we daily increase in faith, hope and charity, but more especially in that charity which is the bond of peace, and perfection of every virtue. May we so practice thy precepts that through the merits of the Redeemer we may finally obtain thy promises, and find an acceptance through the Gates, and into the Temple and City of our God. So mote it be—Amen."

*A Benediction, oftener used at closing than the preceding prayer.*

May the blessing of heaven rest upon us and all regular Masons; may brotherly love prevail, and every moral and social virtue cement us. So mote it be—Amen.

After the prayer the following charge ought to be delivered, but it is seldom attended to; in a majority of lodges it is never attended to.

Master to brethren, "Brethren, we are now about to quit this sacred retreat of friendship and virtue to mix again with the world. Amidst its concerns and employment forget not the duties which you have heard so frequently inculcated, and so forcibly recommended in this lodge. Remember, that around this altar, you have promised to befriend and relieve every brother who shall need your assistance. You have promised in the most friendly manner to remind him of his errors and aid a reformation. These generous principles are to extend further: Every human being has a claim upon your kind offices. Do good unto all. Recommend it more "especially to the household of the faithful." Finally, brethren, be ye all of one mind, live in peace, and may the God of love and peace delight to dwell with and bless you."

In some lodges, after the charge is delivered, the Master says, "Brethren, form on the square." When all the brethren form a circle, and the Master, followed by every brother (except in using the words) says, "And God said let there be light, and there was light." At the same moment that the last of these words drops from the Master's lips, every member stamps with his right foot on the floor, and at the same instant bring their hands together with equal force, and in such perfect unison with each other that persons situated so as to hear it would suppose it the precursor of some dreadful catastrophe. This is called *"the shock."*

Having described all the ceremonies and forms appertaining to the opening of a lodge of Entered Apprentice Masons, setting them to work, initiating a candidate, and closing the lodge, I will now proceed to give the lecture on this degree. It is divided into three sections. The lecture is nothing more or less than a recapitulation of the preceding ceremonies and forms, by way of question and answer, and fully explains the same. In fact, the ceremonies and forms (generally Masonically called *the work*) and lectures are so much the same that he who possesses a knowledge of the lectures cannot be destitute of a knowledge of what the ceremonies and forms are. As the ceremonies used in opening and closing are the same in all the degrees it is thought best to give the whole in one insertion; it being the sincere wish of the writer that every reader should perfectly understand all the formulas of the whole Masonic fabric, as he then will thereby be able to form correct opinions of the propriety or impropriety, advantages or disadvantages of the same.

*First Section of the Lecture on the First Degree of Masonry.*

"From whence come you as an Entered Apprentice Mason?"

Ans. "From the holy lodge of St. John, at Jerusalem."

"What recommendations do you bring?"

Ans. "Recommendations from the Worshipful Master, Wardens and brethren of that right worshipful lodge, whom greet you."

"What comest thou hither to do?"

Ans. "To learn to subdue my passions, and improve myself in the secret arts and mysteries of ancient Freemasonry."

"You are a Mason then, I presume?"

Ans. "I am."

How shall I know you to be a Mason?"

Ans. "By certain signs and a token."

"What are signs ?"

Ans. "All right angles, horizontals and perpendiculars."

"What is a token?"

Ans. "A certain friendly and brotherly grip, whereby one Mason may know another, in the dark as well as in the light."

"Where were you first prepared to be made a Mason?"

Ans. "In my heart."

"Where secondly?"

Ans. "In a room adjacent to the body of a just and lawfully constituted lodge of such."

"How were you prepared?"

Ans. "By being divested of all metals, neither naked nor clothed, barefoot nor shod, hoodwinked, with a Cable Towt about my neck, in which situation I was conducted to the door of the lodge."

"You being hoodwinked how did you know it to be a door?"

Ans. "By first meeting with resistance, and afterwards gaining admission."

"How did you gain admission?"

Ans. "By three distinct knocks from without, answered by the same within."

"What was said to you from within?"

Ans. "Who comes there? Who comes there? Who comes there?

"Your answer?"

Ans. "A poor blind candidate who has long been desirous of having and receiving a part of the rights and benefits of this worshipful lodge, dedicated to God, and held forth to the holy order of St. John, as all true fellows and brothers have done, who have gone this way before me."

"What further was said to you from within?"

Ans. "I was asked if it was of my own free will and accord I made this request, if I was duly and truly proposed, worthy and well qualified, all of which being answered in the affirmative, I was asked by what further rights I ex-

*Three miles long.

pected to obtain so great a favor or benefit."

"Your answer?"

Ans. "By being a man, free born, of lawful age and well recommended."

"What was then said to you?"

Ans. "I was bid to wait till the Worshipful Master in the east was made acquainted with my request and his answer returned."

"After his answer returned what followed?"

Ans. "I was caused to enter the lodge."

"How?"

Ans. "On the point of some sharp instrument pressing my naked left breast in the name of the Lord."

"How were you then disposed of?"

Ans. "I was conducted to the center of the lodge and there caused to kneel for the benefit of a prayer." [See page 19.]

"After prayer what was said to you?"

Ans. "I was asked in whom I put my trust."

"Your answer?"

Ans. "In God."

"What followed?"

Ans. "The Worshipful Master took me by the right hand and said, 'Since in God you put your trust, arise, and follow your leader, and fear no danger.'"

"How were you then disposed of?"

Ans. "I was conducted three times regularly round the lodge and halted at the Junior Warden in the south, where the same questions were asked and answers returned as at the door."

"How did the Junior Warden dispose of you?"

Ans. "He ordered me to be conducted to the Senior Warden in the west; where the same questions were asked and answers returned as before."

"How did the Senior Warden dispose of you?"

Ans. "He ordered me to be conducted to the Worshipful Master in the east, where the same questions were asked and answers returned as before, who likewise demanded of me from whence I came and whither I was traveling."

"Your answer?"

Ans. "From the west and traveling to the east."

"Why do you leave the west and travel to the east?"

Ans. "In search of light."

"How did the Worshipful Master then dispose of you?"

Ans. "He ordered me to be conducted back to the west, from whence I came, and put in the care of the Senior Warden, who taught me how to approach the east, the place of light, by advancing upon one upright regular step to the first step, my feet forming the right angle of an oblong square, my body erect at the altar before the Worshipful Master."

"What did the Worshipful Master do with you?"

Ans. "He made an Entered Apprentice Mason of me."

"How?"

Ans. "In due form."

"What was that due form?"

Ans. "My left knee bare, bent, my right forming a square; my left hand supporting the Holy Bible, Square, and Compass, and my right covering the same; in which position I took upon me the solemn oath or obligation of an Entered Apprentice Mason. [See page 21.]

"After you had taken your obligation what was said to you?"

Ans. "I was asked what I most desired."

"Your answer?"

Ans. "Light."

"Were you immediately brought to light?"

Ans. "I was."

"How?"

Ans. "By the direction of the Master and assistance of the brethren."

"What did you first discover after being brought to light?"

Ans. "Three great lights in Masonry, by the assistance of three lesser."

"What were those three great lights in Masonry?"

Ans. "The Holy Bible, Square and Compass."

"How are they explained?"

Ans. "The Holy Bible is given to us as a guide for our faith and practice; the Square to square our actions; and the Compass to keep us in due bounds with all mankind, but more especially with the brethren."

may know another in the dark as well as the light."

"What were those three lesser lights?"

Ans. "Three burning tapers, or candle, on **candle** sticks."

"What do they represent?"

Ans. "The Sun, Moon, and Master of the lodge."

"How are they explained?"

Ans. "As the Sun rules the day, and the Moon governs the night, so ought the Worshipful Master to use his endeavors to rule and govern his lodge with equal regularity or cause the same to be done."

"What did you next discover?"

Ans. "The Worshipful Master approaching me from the east, under the sign and due-guard of an Entered Apprentice Mason, who presented me with his right hand in token of brotherly love and esteem, and proceeded to give me the grip and word of an Entered Apprentice Mason, and bid me arise and salute the Junior and Senior Wardens and convince them that I had been regularly initiated as an Entered Apprentice Mason, and was in possession of the sign, grip and word."

"What did you next discover?"

Ans. "The Worshipful Master a second time approaching me from the east, who presented me with a lambskin or white apron, which he said was an emblem of innocence, and the badge of a Mason; that it had been worn by kings, princes and potentates of the earth who had never been ashamed to wear it; that it was more honorable than the diadems of kings or pearls of princesses, when worthily worn, and more ancient than the Golden Fleece, or Roman Eagle, more honorable than the Star or Garter, or any other order that could be conferred upon me at that time or any time thereafter, except it be in the body of a just and lawfully constituted lodge of Masons; and bid me carry it to the Senior Warden in the west, who taught me how to wear it as an Entered Apprentice Mason."

"What were you next presented with?"

Ans. "The working tools of an Entered Apprentice Mason."

"What were they?"

Ans. "A twenty-four inch gauge and common gavel."

"How were they explained?"

Ans. "The twenty-four inch gauge is an instrument made use of by operative masons to measure and lay out their work, but we as Free and Accepted Masons are taught to make use of it for the more noble and glorious purpose of dividing our time; the twenty-four inches on the gauge are emblematical of the twenty-four hours in the day, which we are taught to divide into three equal parts, whereby we find eight hours for the service of God and a worthy distressed brother, eight hours for our usual vocation, and eight hours for refreshment and sleep. The common gavel is an instrument made use of by operative masons to break off the corners of rough stones, the better to fit them for the builder's use, but we, as Free and Accepted Masons, are taught to make use of it for the more noble and glorious purpose of divesting our hearts and consciences of all the vices and superfluities of life, thereby fitting our minds as lively and living stones for that spiritual building, that House not made with hands, eternal in the heavens."

"What were you next presented with?"

Ans. "A new name."

"What was that?"

Ans. "Caution."

"What does it teach?"

Ans. "It teaches me as I was barely instructed in the rudiments of Masonry, that I should be cautious over all my words and actions, especially when before its enemies."

"What were you next presented with?"

Ans. "Three precious jewels."

"What are they?"

Ans. "A listening ear, a silent tongue, and a faithful heart."

"What do they teach?"

Ans. "A listening ear teaches me to listen to the instructions of the Worshipful Master, but more especially that I should listen to the calls and cries of a worthy distressed brother. A silent tongue teaches me to be silent in the lodge, that the peace and harmony thereof may not be disturbed; but more especially that I should be silent when before the enemies of Masonry. A faithful heart, that I should be faithful to the instructions of the Worshipful Master at all times, but more especially that I should be faithful and keep and conceal the secrets of Masonry, and those of a brother, when given to me in charge as such, that they remain as secure and inviolable in my breast, as in his own before communicated to me."

"What were you next presented with?"

Ans. "Check-words two."

"What were they?"

Ans. "Truth and Union."

"How explained?"

"Truth is a divine attribute, and the foundation of every virtue. To be good and true are the first lessons we are taught in Masonry. On this theme we contemplate, and by its dictates endeavor to regulate our conduct; hence, while influenced by this principle, hypocrisy and deceit are unknown amongst us; sincerity and plain dealing distinguishes us; and heart and tongue join in promoting each other's welfare, and rejoicing in each other's prosperity. Union is that kind of friendship that ought to appear conspicuous in the conduct of every Mason. It is so closely allied to the divine attribute, truth, that he who enjoys the one is seldom destitute of the other. Should interest, honor, prejudice, or human depravity ever influence you to violate any part of the sacred trust we now repose in you, let these two important words, at the earliest insinuation, teach you to put on the check-line of truth, which will infallibly direct you to pursue that strait and narrow path, which ends in the full enjoyment of the Grand Lodge above, where we shall all meet as Masons and members of one family; where all discord on account of religion, politics or private opinion shall be unknown and banished from within our walls."

"What followed?"

Ans. "The Worshipful Master in the east made a demand of me something of a metalic kind, which he said was not so much on account of its intrinsic value, as that it might be deposited in the archives of the lodge, as a memorial that I had therein been made a Mason."

"How did the Worshipful Master then dispose of you?"

"He ordered me to be conducted out of the lodge and vested of what I had been divested, and returned for further instructions."

"After you returned how were you disposed of."

Ans. "I was conducted to the northeast corner of the lodge, and there caused to stand upright like a man, my feet forming a square, and received a solemn injunction, ever to walk and act uprightly before God and man, and in addition thereto, received the following charge: [For this charge see page 27.]

## SECTION SECOND.

"Why was you divested of all metals when you was made a Mason?"

Ans. "Because Masonry regards no man on account of his worldly wealth or honors; it is, therefore, the internal and not the external qualifications that recommend a man to Masonry."

"A second reason?"

Ans. "There was neither the sound of an axe, hammer, or any other metal tool heard at the building of King Soloman's temple."

"How could so stupendous a fabric be erected without the sound of axe, hammer, or any other metal tool?"

Ans. "All the stones were hewed, squared and numbered in the quarries where they were raised, all the timbers felled and prepared in the forests of Lebanon, and carried down to Joppa on floats, and taken from thence up to Jerusalem, and set up with wooden mauls, prepared for that purpose; which, when completed, every part thereof fitted with that exact nicety, that it had more the resemblance of the hand workmanship of the Supreme Architect of the Universe, than that of human hands."

"Why was you neither naked nor clothed?"

Ans. "As I was an object of distress at that time, it was to remind me, if ever I saw a friend, more especially a brother, in a like distressed situation, that I should contribute as liberally to his relief as his situation required, and my abilities would admit, without material injury to myself or family."

"Why were you neither barefoot or shod?"

Ans. "It was an ancient Israelitish custom, adopted among Masons; and we read, in the book of Ruth, concerning their mode and manner of changing and redeeming, 'and to confirm all things, a brother plucked off his shoe and gave it to his neighbor, and that was testimony in Israel.' This, then, therefore, we do in confirmation of a token and as a pledge of our fidelity; thereby signifying that we will renounce our own wills in all things, and become obedient to the laws of our ancient institutions."

"Why were you hoodwinked?"

"That my heart might conceive before my eyes beheld the beauties of Masonry."

"A second reason?"

Ans. "As I was in darkness at that time, it was to remind me that I should keep the whole world so respecting Masonry."

"Why had you a Cable Tow about your neck?"

Ans. "In case I had not submitted to the manner and mode of my initiation, that I might have been led out of the lodge without seeing the form and beauties thereof."

"Why did you give three distinct knocks at the door?"

Ans. "To alarm the lodge, and let the Worshipful Master, Wardens and brethren know that a poor blind candidate prayed admission."

"What does those three distinct knocks allude to?"

Ans. "A certain passage in Scripture, wherein it says, 'Ask and it shall be given, seek and ye shall find, knock and it shall be opened unto you.' "

"How did you apply this to your then case in Masonry?"

Ans. "I asked the recommendations of a friend to become a Mason, I sought admission through his recommendations, and knocked, and the door of Masonry opened unto me."

"Why was you caused to enter on the point of some sharp instrument pressing your naked left breast in the name of the Lord?"

Ans. "As this was a torture to my flesh, so might the recollection of it ever be to my heart and conscience, if ever I attempted to reveal the secrets of Masonry unlawfully."

"Why was you conducted to the center of the lodge, and there caused to kneel for the benefit of a prayer?"

Ans. "Before entering on this, or any other great and important undertaking, it is highly necessary to implore a blessing from Deity."

"Why was you asked in whom you put your trust?"

Ans. "Agreeable to the laws of our ancient institution, no atheist could be made a Mason, it was therefore necessary that I should believe in Deity; otherwise no oath or obligation could bind me."

"Why did the Worshipful Master take you by the right hand and bid you arise, follow your leader and fear no danger?"

Ans. "As I was in darkness at that time, and could neither foresee nor avoid danger, it was to remind me that I was in the hands of an affectionate friend, in whose fidelity I might with safety confide."

"Why was you conducted three times regularly round the lodge?"

Ans. "That the Worshipful Master, Wardens and brethren might see that I was duly and truly prepared."

"Why did you meet with those several obstructions on the way?"

Ans. "This and every lodge is, or ought to be, a true representation of King Solomon's Temple, which, when completed, had guards stationed at the east, west and south gates."

"Why had they guards stationed at those several gates?"

Ans. "To prevent any one from passing or repassing that was not duly qualified."

"Why did you kneel on your left knee and not on your right, or both?"

Ans. "The left side has ever been considered the weakest part of the body; it was therefore to remind me that the part I was then taking upon me was the weakest part of Masonry, it being that only of an Entered Apprentice."

"Why was your right hand placed on the Holy Bible, Square and Compass, and not your left, or both?"

Ans. "The right hand has ever been considered the seat of fidelity, and our ancient brethren worshiped Deity under the name of FIDES, which has sometimes been represented by two right hands joined together; at others, by two human figures holding each other by the right hand; the right hand. therefore, we use in this great and important undertaking to signify, in the strongest manner possible, the sincerity of our intentions in the business we are engaged.

"Why did the Worshipful Master present you with a lambskin or white apron?"

Ans. "The lambskin has, in all ages, been deemed an emblem of innocence; he, therefore, who wears the lambskin, as a badge of a Mason, is thereby continually reminded of that purity of life and rectitude of conduct which is so essentially necessary to our gaining admission into the celestial lodge above, where the Supreme Architect of the Universe presides."

"Why did the Master make a demand of you of something of a metallic nature?"

Ans. "As I was in a poor and pennyless situation at that time, it was to remind me if ever I saw a friend, but more especially a brother, in the like poor and pennyless situation, that I should contribute as liberally to his relief as my abilities would admit and his situation required, without injuring myself or family."

"Why was you conducted to the northeast corner of the lodge, and there caused to stand upright like a man, your feet forming a square, receiving at the same time a solemn charge ever to walk and act upright before God and man?"

Ans. "The first stone in every Masonic edifice is, or ought to be placed at the northeast corner, that being the place where an Entered Apprentice Mason receives his first instructions to build his future Masonic edifice upon."


## THIRD SECTION.


"We have been saying a good deal about a lodge; I want to know what constitutes a lodge?"

Ans. "A certain number of Free and Accepted Masons duly assembled in a room, or place, with the Holy Bible,

Square and Compass, and other Masonic implements **with** a charter from the Grand Lodge empowering them **to** work."

"Where did our ancient brethren meet before lodges were erected?"

Ans. "On the highest hills, and in the lowest vales."

"Why on the highest hills and the lowest vales?"

Ans. "The better to guard against cowans and enemies, either ascending or descending, that the brethren might have timely notice of their approach to prevent being surprised."

"What is the form of your lodge?"

Ans. "An oblong square."

"How long?"

Ans. "From east to west."

"How wide?"

Ans. "Between north and south."

"How high?"

Ans. "From the surface of the earth to the highest heavens."

"How deep?"

Ans. "From the surface to the center."

"What supports your lodge?"

Ans. "Three large columns or pillars."

"What are their names?"

Ans. "Wisdom, Strength and Beauty."

"Why so?"

Ans. "It is necessary there should be wisdom to contrive, strength to support, and beauty to adorn all great and important undertakings, but more especially this of ours."

"Has your lodge any covering?"

Ans. "It has; a clouded canopy, or a starry decked heaven, where all good Masons hope to arrive."

"How do they hope to arrive there?"

Ans. "By the assistance of Jacob's ladder."

"How many principal rounds has it got?"

Ans. "Three."

"What are their names?"

Ans. "Faith, Hope and Charity."

"What do they teach?"

Ans. "Faith in God, Hope in immortality, and Charity to all mankind."

"Has your lodge any furniture?"

Ans. "It has; the Holy Bible, Square, and Compass."

"To whom do they belong?"

Ans. "The Bible to God, the Square to the Master, and the Compass to the Craft."

"How explained?"

Ans. "The Bible to God, it being the inestimable gift of God to man, for his instruction to guide him through the rugged paths of life; the Square to the Master, it being the proper emblem of his office; the Compass to the Craft, by a due attention to which we are taught to limit our desires, curb our ambition, subdue our irregular appetites, and keep our passions and prejudices in due bonds with all mankind, but more especially with the brethren."

"Has your lodge any ornaments?"

Ans. "It has; the mosaic, or chequered pavement, the indented tessels, the beautiful tessellated border which surrounds it, with the blazing star in the center."

"What do they represent?"

Ans. "Mosaic or chequered pavement represents this world, which, though chequered over with good and evil, yet brethren may walk together thereon and not stumble; the indented tessel, with the blazing star in the center, the manifold blessings and comforts with which we are surrounded in this life, but more especially those which we hope to enjoy hereafter; the blazing star, that prudence which ought to appear conspicuous in the conduct of every Mason, but more especially commemorative of the star which appeared in the east, to guide the wise men to Bethlehem, to proclaim the birth and the presence of the Son of God."

"Has your lodge any lights?"

Ans. "It has three."

"How are they situated?"

Ans. "East, west, and south."

"Has it none in the north?"

Ans. "It has not."

"Why so?"

Ans. "Because this and every other lodge is, or ought to be a true representation of King Solomon's Temple, which was situated north of the ecliptic; the sun and moon there-fore darting their rays from the south, no light was to be expected from the north; we, therefore, Masonically, term the north a place of darkness."

"Has your lodge any jewels?"

Ans. "It has six; three movable and three immovable."

"What are the three movable jewels?"

Ans. "The Square, Level, and Plumb."

"What do they teach?"

Ans. "The Square, morality; the Level, equality; and the Plumb, rectitude of life and conduct."

"What are the three immovable jewels?"

Ans. "The rough Ashlar, the perfect Ashlar, and the Trestle-board."

"What are they?"

Ans. "The rough Ashlar is a stone in its rough and natural state; the perfect Ashlar is also a stone made ready by the working tool of the Fellow Craft to be adjusted in the building; and the Trestle-board is for the master workman to draw his plans and designs upon."

"What do they represent?"

Ans. "The rough Ashlar represents man in his rude and imperfect state by nature; the perfect Ashlar also represents man in that state of perfection to which we all hope to arrive by means of a virtuous life and education, our own endeavors, and the blessing of God. In erecting our temporal building we pursue the plans and designs laid down by the master workman on his Trestle-board; but in erecting our spiritual building we pursue the plans and designs laid down by the supreme Geometrician of the universe, in the book of life, which we Masonically term our spiritual Trestle-board."

"Who did you serve?"

Ans. "My Master."

"How long?"

Ans. "Six days."

"What did you serve him with?"

Ans. "Freedom, fervency, and zeal."

"What do they represent?"

Ans. "Chalk, charcoal, and earth."

"Why so?"

Ans. "There is nothing freer than chalk, the slightest touch of which leaves a trace behind; nothing more fervent than heated charcoal, it will melt the most obdurate metals; nothing more zealous than the earth to bring forth."

"How is your lodge situated?"

Ans. "Due east and west."

"Why so?"

Ans. "Because the sun rises in the east and sets in the west."

"A second reason?"

Ans. "The gospel was first preached in the east, and is spreading to the west."

"A third reason?"

Ans. "The liberal arts and sciences began in the east and are extending to the west."

"A fourth reason?"

Ans. "Because all Churches and Chapels are, or ought to be, so situated."

"Why are all Churches and Chapels so situated?"

Ans. "Because king Solomon's temple was so situated."

"Why was king Solomon's temple so situated?"

Ans. "Because Moses, after conducting the children of Israel through the Red Sea, by Divine command erected a tabernacle to God, and placed it due east and west; which was to commemorate, to the latest posterity, that miraculous east wind that wrought their deliverance; and this was an exact model of king Solomon's temple. Since which time every well regulated and governed lodge is, or ought to be, so situated."

"To whom did our ancient brethren dedicate their lodges?"

Ans. "To king Solomon."

"Why so?"

Ans. "Because king Solomon was our most ancient Grand Master."

"To whom do modern Masons dedicate their lodges?"

Ans. "To St. John the Baptist and St. John the Evangelist."

"Why so?"

Ans. "Because they were the two most ancient Christian patrons of Masonry; and since their time, in every well regulated & governed lodge there has been a certain point within a circle, which circle is bounded on the east and the west by two perpendicular and parallel lines, representing the anniversary of St. John the Baptist, and St. John the Evangelist, who were two perfect parallels, as well in Masonry as Christianity; on the vertex of which rests the book of the Holy Scriptures, supporting Jacob's ladder, which is said to reach the watery clouds; and in passing round this circle we naturally touch on both these perpendicular parallel lines, as well as the book of the Holy Scriptures, and while a Mason keeps himself thus circumscribed he cannot materially err."

[Thus ends the first degree of Masonry, and the reader who has read and paid attention to it knows more of Masonry than any Entered Apprentice Mason in christendom, and more of this degree than one hundredth part of the Master Masons, or even Royal Arch Masons; for very few ever attempt to learn the lectures, or even the obligations; they merely receive the degrees, and there stop, with the exception of a few who are fascinated with the idea of holding an office; they sometimes endeavor to qualify themselves to discharge the duties which devolve upon them in their respective offices The offices of secretary and treasurer are by some considered the most important in the lodge, particularly where there is much business done.]

## SECOND OR FELLOW CRAFT DEGREE.

I will now introduce the reader to the second degree of Masonry. It is generally called passing, as will be seen in the lecture. I shall omit the ceremonies of opening and closing, as they are precisely the same as in the first degree, except two knocks are used in this degree, and the door is entered by the benefit of a pass-word. It is SHIBBOLETH. It will be explained in the lecture.

The candidate, as before, is taken into the preparation room, and prepared in the manner following:

Dress of Fellow Craft.

All his clothing taken off, except his shirt; furnished with a pair of drawers; his right b. east bare; his left foot in a slipper, his right bare; a cable-tow twice around his neck; semi-hood-winked; in which situation he is conducted to the door of the lodge, where he gives two knocks, when the Senior Deacon rises and says: "Worshipful, while we are peacably at work on the second degree of Masonry, under the influence of faith, hope, and charity, the door of the lodge is alarmed." Master to Senior Deacon, "Enquire the cause of that alarm." [In many lodges they come to the door, knock, are answered by the Senior Deacon, and come in without their being noticed by the Senior Warden or Master.] The Senior Deacon gives two raps on the inside of the door. The candidate gives one without; it is answered by the Senior Deacon with one, when the door is partly opened by the Senior Deacon, who enquires, "Who comes here? Who comes here?

Note.—In modern lodges both eyes are covered, and the cable-tow is put around the naked right arm, instead of around the neck. See cut.

The Junior Deacon, who is or ought to be the conductor, answers, "A worthy brother who has bee. regularly initiated as an Entered Apprentice Mason, served a proper time as such, and now wishes for further light in Masonry by being passed to the degree of Fellow Craft."

Senior Deacon to Junior Deacon. "Is it of his own free will and accord he makes this request?"

Ans. "It is."

Senior Deacon to Junior Deacon: "Is he duly and truly prepared?"

Ans. "He is."

Senior Deacon to Junior Deacon. "Is he worthy and well qualified?"

Ans. "He is."

Senior Deacon to Junior Deacon. "Has he made suitable proficiency in the preceding degree?"

Ans. "He has."

[Very few know any more than they did the night they were initiated, have not heard their obligation repeated, nor one section of the lecture, and in fact a very small proportion of Masons ever learn either.]

Senior Deacon to Junior Deacon. "By what further rights does he expect to obtain this benefit?"

Ans. "By the benefit of a pass-word."

Senior Deacon to Junior Deacon. "Has he a pass-word?"

Ans. "He has not, but I have it for him."

Senior Deacon to Junior Deacon. "Give it to me."

The Junior Deacon whispers in the Senior Deacon's ear, "Shibboleth."

The Senior Deacon says, "The pass is right; since this is the case, you will wait till the Worshipful Master in the east is made acquainted with his request, and his answer returned."

The Senior Deacon then repairs to the Master and gives two knocks, as at the door, which are answered by two by the Master, when the same questions are asked, and answers returned as at the door, after which the Master says, "Since he comes with all these necessary qualifications, let him enter this Worshipful Lodge in the name of the Lord and take heed on what he enters." As he enters, the angle of the square is pressed hard against his naked right breast, ιt which time the Senior Deacon says, "Brother, when you ιntered this lodge the first time, you entered on the point ιf the compass pressing your naked left breast, which was hen explained to you. You now enter it on the angle of the ιquare pressing your naked right breast, which is to teach ιou to act upon the square with all mankind, but more ιspecially with the brethren." The candidate is then conducted twice regularly round the lodge, and halted at the Junior Warden in the south, where he gives two raps, and is answered by two, when the same questions are asked, and answers returned as at the door; from thence he is conducted to the Senior Warden, where the same questions are asked and answers returned as before; he is then conducted to the Master in the east, where the same questions are asked and answers returned as before; the Master likewise demands of him from whence he came and whither he is traveling.

He answers, "From the west, and traveling to the east."

The Master asks, "Why do you leave the west and travel to the east?"

Ans. "In search of more light."

The Master then says to the conductor, "Since this is the case, you will please conduct the candidate back to the west from whence he came, and put him in care of the Senior Warden, who will teach him how to approach the east, the place of light, by advancing upon two upright regular steps to the second step [his heel is in the hollow of the right foot on this degree], his feet forming the right angle of an oblong square, and his body erect at the altar before the Worshipful Master, and place him in a proper position to take the solemn oath or obligation of a Fellow Craft Mason."

The Master then leaves his seat and approaches the kneeling candidate [the candidate kneels on the right knee, the left forming a square, his left arm as far as the elbow in a horizontal position, and the rest of the arm in a vertical position so as to form a square, his arm supported by the square held under his elbow] and says, "Brother, you are now placed in a proper position to take on you the solemn oath or obligation of a Fellow Craft Mason, which I assure you as before is neither to affect your religion nor politics; if you are willing to take it, repeat your name and say after me":

"I, A. B., of my own free will and accord, in the presence of Almighty God, and this worshipful lodge of Fellow Craft Masons, dedicated to God, and held forth to the holy order of St. John, do hereby and hereon most solemnly and sincerely promise and swear, in addition to my former obligation, that I will not give the degree of a Fellow Craft Mason to any one of an inferior degree, nor to any other being in the known world, except it be to a true and lawful brother or brethren Fellow Craft Masons, within the body of a just and lawfully constituted lodge of such; and not unto him nor unto them, whom I shall hear so to be, but unto him and them only whom I shall find so to be after strict trial and due examination or lawful information. Furthermore do I promise and swear that I will not wrong this lodge nor a brother of this degree to the value of two cents, knowingly, myself, nor suffer it to be done by others if in my power to prevent it. Furthermore do I promise and swear that I will support the Constitution of the Grand Lodge of the United States, and of the Grand Lodge of this State, under which this lodge is held, and conform to all the by-laws, rules, and regulations of this or any other lodge of which I may at any time hereafter become a member, as far as in my power. Furthermore, do I promise and swear that I will obey all regular signs and summonses given, handed, sent, or thrown to me by the hand of a brother Fellow Craft Mason, or from the body of a just and lawfully constituted lodge of such, provided that it be within the length of my cable-tow, or square and angle of my work. Furthermore, do I promise and swear that I will be aiding and assisting all poor and penniless brethren Fellow Crafts, their widows and orphans, wheresoever disposed round the globe, they applying to me as such, as far as in my power without injuring myself or family. To all which I do most solemnly and sincerely promise and swear without the least hesitation, mental reservation, or self evasion of mind in me whatever; binding myself under no less penalty than to have my left breast torn open and my heart and vitals taken from thence and thrown over my left shoulder and carried into the valley of Jehosaphat, there to become a prey to the wild beasts of the field, and vulture of the air, if ever I should prove willfully guilty of violating any part of this my solemn oath or obligation of a Fellow Craft Mason; so help me God, and keep me steadfast in the due performance of the same."

"Detach your hands and kiss the book which is the Holy Bible, twice." The bandage is now (by one of the brethren) dropped over the other eye, and the Master says, "Brother [at the same time laying his hand on the top of the candidate's head], what do you most desire?"

The candidate answers after his prompter, "More light."

The Master says, "Brethren, form on the square and assist in bringing our new made brother from darkness to light. 'And God said let there be light, and there was light.'" At this instant all the brethren clap their hands and stamp on the floor as in the preceding degree. The Master says to the candidate, "Brother, what do you discover different from before?" The Master says after a short pause, "You now discover one point of the compass elevated above the square, which donates light in this degree; but as one is yet in obscurity, it is to remind you that you are yet one material point in the dark respecting Masonry." The Master steps off from the candidate three or four steps, and says, Brother, you now discover me as master of this lodge approaching you from the east, under the sign and due-guard of a Fellow Craft Mason; do as I do as near as you can and keep your position." The sign is given by drawing your right hand flat, with the palm of it next to your breast, across your breast from the left to the right side with some quickness, and dropping it down by your side; the due-guard is given by raising the left arm until that part of it between the elbow and shoulder is perfectly horizontal, and raising the rest of the arm in a vertical position, so that that part of the arm below the elbow and that part above it form a square. This is called the the due-guard of a Fellow Craft Mason. The

Due Guard.
Fellow Craft. two given together, are called the signs and due-guard of a Fellow Craft Mason, and they are never given separately; they would not be recognized by a Mason if given separately. The Master, by the time he gives his steps, signs. and due-guard, arrives at the candidate

and says, "Brother, I now present you with my right hand, in token of brotherly love and confidence, and with it the pass-grip and word of a Fellow Craft Mason." The pass, or more properly the pass-grip, is given by taking each other by the right hand, as though going to shake hands, and each putting his thumb between the fore and second fingers where they join the hand, and pressing the thumb between the joints. This is the pass-grip of a Fellow Craft Mason, the name of it is Shibboleth. Its origin will be explained in the lecture; the pass-grip some give without lettering or syllabling, and others give it in the same way they do the real grip; the real grip of a Fellow Craft Mason is given by putting the thumb on the joint of the second finger where it joins the hand, and crooking your thumb so that each can stick the nail of his thumb into the joint of the other; this is the real grip of a Fellow Craft Mason; the name of it is Jachin, it is given in the following manner: If you wish to examine a person after having taken each other by the grip, ask him, "What is this?"

Ans. "A grip."

"A grip of what?"

Ans. "The grip of a Fellow Craft Mason."

"Has it a name?"

Ans. "It has.

"Will you give it to me?"

Ans. "I did not so receive it, neither can I so impart it."

"What will you do with it?"

Ans. "I'll letter it or halve it."

"Halve it and you begin."

Ans. "No, begin you."

"You begin."

Ans. "J A."

CHIN."

Ans. "JACHIN."

"Right, brother, Jachin, I greet you."

As the signs, due-guards, grips, words, pass-words, and their several names comprise pretty much all the secrets of Masonry, and all the information necessary to pass us as Masons, I intend to appropriate a few passages in the latter part of this work to the exclusive purpose of explaining them; I shall not, therefore, spend much time in examining them as I progress. After the Master gives the candidate the pass-grip and grip, and their names, he says, "Brother, you will rise and salute the Junior and Senior Wardens, as such, and convince them that you have been regularly passed to the degree of a Fellow Craft Mason, and have got the sign and pass-grip, real grip and their names." [I do not here express it as expressed in lodges generally; the Master generally says, "You will arise and salute the Wardens, &c, and convince them, &c., that you have got the sign, pass-grip, and word." It is obviously wrong, because the first thing he gives is the sign, then due-guard, then the pass-grip, real grip, and their names.] While the Wardens are examining the candidate, the Master gets an apron, and returns to the candidate, and says, "Brother, I now have the honor of presenting you with a lambskin or white apron as before, which I hope you will continue to wear with honor to yourself and satisfaction to the brethren; you will please carry it to the Senior Warden in the west, who will teach you how to wear it as a Fellow Craft Mason." The Senior Warden ties on his apron and turns up one corner of the lower end of the apron and tucks it under the apron string. The Senior Deacon then conducts his pupil to the Master, who has by this time resumed his seat in the east, where he has, or ought to have, the floor carpet to assist him in his explanations. Master to the candidate, "Brother, as you are dressed, it is necessary you should have tools to work with. I will therefore present you with the tools of a Fellow Craft Mason. They are the plumb, square, and level. The plumb is an instrument made use of by operative Masons to raise perpendiculars, the square to square their work, and the level to lay horizontals, but we, as Free and Accepted Masons, are taught to use them for a more noble and glorious purpose; the plumb teaches us to walk uprightly in our several stations before God and man, squaring our actions by the square of virtue, and remembering that we are traveling on the level of time to that undiscovered country from whose bourne no traveler has returned. I further present you with three precious jewels; their names are Faith, Hope, and Charity; they teach us to have faith in God, hope in immortality, and charity to all mankind." The Master to the Senior Deacon, "You will now conduct the candidate out of the lodge and invest him of what he has been divested." After he is clothed and the necessary arrangements made for his reception, such as placing the columns and floor carpet, if they have any, and the candidate is reconducted back to the lodge; as he enters the door the Senior Deacon observes, "We are now about to return to the middle chamber of King Solomon's temple." When within the door the Senior Deacon proceeds, "Brother, we have worked in speculative Masonry, but our forefathers wrought both in speculative and operative Masonry; they worked at the building of King Solomon's temple, and many other Masonic edifices; they wrought six days; they did not work on the seventh, because in six days God created the heavens and earth and rested on the seventh day; the seventh, therefore, our ancient brethren consecrated as a day of rest, thereby enjoying more frequent opportunities to contemplate the glorious works of creation and to adore their great Creator." Moving a step or two, the Senior Deacon proceeds, "Brother, the first thing that attracts our attention are two large columns, or pillars, one on the left hand and the other on the right; the name of the one on the left hand is Boaz, and denotes strength; the name of the one on the right hand is Jachin, and denotes establishment; they collectively allude to a passage in Scripture wherein God has declared in his word, 'In strength shall this House be established.'"

These columns are eighteen cubits high, twelve in circumference, and four in diameter; they are adorned with two large Chapiters, one on each, and these Chapiters are ornamented with net-work, lily-work, and pomegranates; they denote unity, peace, and plenty. The net-work, from its connection, denotes union, the lily, from its whiteness, purity and peace, and the pomegranate, from the exuberance of its seed, denotes plenty. They also have two large globes or balls, one on each; these globes or balls contain on their convex surface all the maps and charts of the celestial and ter restrial bodies; they are said to be thus extensive to denote the universality of Masonry, and that a Mason's charity ought to be equally extensive. Their composition is molten, or cast brass; they were cast on the river Jordan, in the clay ground, between Succoth and Zaradatha, where King Solomon ordered these and all other holy vessels to be cast; they were cast hollow, and were four inches, or a hand-breadth, thick; they were cast hollow better to withstand inundations and conflagrations, were the archives of Masonry, and contained the constitution, rolls, and records." The Senior Deacon having explained the columns, he passes between them, advancing a step or two, observing as he advances, "Brother, we will pursue our travels; the next that we come to is a long, winding staircase, with three, five, seven steps, or more." The first three allude to the three principal supports in Masonry, viz.: wisdom, strength, and beauty; the five steps allude to the five orders in architecture, and the five human senses; the five orders in architecture are the Tuscan, Doric, Ionic, Corinthian, and Composite; the five human senses are hearing, seeing, feeling, smelling, and tasting, the first three of which have ever been highly essential among Masons— hearing, to hear the word; seeing, to see the sign; feeling, to feel the grip whereby one Mason may know another in the dark as well as in the light. The seven steps allude to the seven sabbatical years, seven years of famine, seven years in building the temple, seven golden candlesticks, seven wonders of the world, seven planets, but more especially the seven liberal arts and sciences, which are grammar, rhetoric, logic, arithmetic, geometry, music, and astronomy; for this and many other reasons the number seven has ever been held in high estimation among Masons. Advancing a few steps, the Senior Deacon proceeds, "Brother, the next thing we come to is the outer door of the middle chamber of King Solomon's temple, which is partly open, but closely tyled by the Junior Warden." [It is the Junior Warden in the south, who represents the Tyler at the outer door of the middle chamber of King Solomon's temple], who on the approach of the Senior Deacon and candidate enquires, "Who comes here? Who comes here?"

The Senior Deacon answers, "A Fellow Craft Mason."

Junior Warden to Senior Deacon, "How do you expect to gain admission?"

Ans. "By a pass, and token of a pass."

Junior Warden to Senior Deacon, "Will you give them to me?"

The Senior Deacon or the candidate (prompted by him) gives them; this and many other tokens and grips are frequently given by strangers, when first introduced to each other. If given to a Mason he will immediately return it; they can be given by any company unobserved, even by Masons, when shaking hands. A pass and token of a pass; the pass is the word Shibboleth; the token, alias the pass-grip is given as before described, by taking each other by the right hand, as if shaking hands, and placing thumb between the forefinger and the second finger at the third joint, or where they join the hand, and pressing it hard enough to attract attention. In the lecture it is called a token, but generally called the pass-grip; it is an undeniable fact that Masons express themselves so differently, when they mean the same thing, that they frequently wholly misunderstand each other.

After the Junior Warden has received the pass, Shibboleth, he enquires, "What does it denote?

Ans. "Plenty."

Junior Warden to Senior Deacon, "Why so?"

Ans. "From an ear of corn being placed at the water ford."

Junior Warden to Senior Deacon, "Why was this pass instituted?"

"In consequence of a quarrel, which had long existed between Jeptha, judge of Israel, and the Ephraimites, the latter of whom had long been a stubborn, rebellious people, whom Jeptha had endeavored to subdue by lenient measures, but to no effect. The Ephraimites, being highly incensed against Jeptha for not being called to fight and share in the rich spoils of the Amonitish war, assembled a mighty army and passed over the river Jordan to give Jeptha battle; but he, being apprised of their approach, called together the men of Israel, and put them to flight; and, to make his victory more complete, he ordered guards to be placed at the different passes on the banks of the river Jordan and commanded, if the Ephraimites passed that way, that they should pronounce the word Shibboleth, but they, being of a different tribe, pro nounced it Seboleth, which trifling defect proved them spies, and cost them their lives; and there fell that day at the different passes on the banks of the river Jordan forty and two thousand. This word was also used by our ancient brethren to distinguish a friend from a foe, and has since been adopted as a proper pass-word, to be given before entering any well regulated and governed lodge of Fellow Craft Masons." "Since this is the case, you will pass on to the Senior Warden in the west for further examination." As they approach the Senior Warden in the west, the Senior Deacon says to the candidate, "Brother, the next thing we come to is the inner door of the middle chamber of King Solomon's temple, which we find partly open, but more closely tyled by the Senior Warden," when the Senior Warden enquires, "Who comes here? Who comes here?"

The Senior Deacon answers, "A Fellow Craft Mason."

Senior Warden to Senior Deacon, "How do you expect to gain admission?"

Ans. "By the grip and word."

The Senior Warden to the Senior Deacon, "Will you give them to me?"

They are then given as herein before described. The word is Jachin. After they are given the Senior Warden says, "They are right, you can pass on to the Worshipful Master in the east." As they approach the Master, he enquires, "Who comes here? Who comes here?"

Senior Deacon answers, "A Fellow Craft Mason."

The Master then says to the candidate, "Brother, you have been admitted into the middle chamber of King Solomon's temple for the sake of the letter G. It denotes Deity, before whom we all ought to bow in reverence, worship and adore. It also denotes Geometry, the fifth science, it being that on which this degree was principally founded. By Geometry we may curiously trace nature through her various windings to her most concealed recesses. By it we may discover the power, the wisdom, and the goodness of the Grand Artificer of the universe, and view with delight the proportions which connect this vast machine. By it we may discover how the planets move in their orbits, and demonstrate their various revolutions. By it we may account for the return of seasons, and the variety of scenes which each season displays to the discerning eye. Numberless worlds surround us, all formed by the same Divine Architect, which roll through the vast expanse, and all conducted by the same unerring law of nature. A survey of nature, and the observations of her beautiful proportions first determined man to imitate the divine plan, and study symmetry and order. The architect began to design; and the plans which he laid down, being improved by experience and time, have produced works which are the admiration of every age. The lapse of time, the ruthless hand of ignorance, and the devastations of war have laid waste and destroyed many valuable monuments of antiquity on which the utmost exertions of human genius have been employed. Even the temple of Solomon, so spacious and magnificent, and constructed by so many celebrated artists, escaped not the unsparing ravages of barbarous force. The attentive ear receives the sound from the instructive tongue; and the mysteries of Freemasonry are safely lodged in the repository of faithful breasts. Tools and implements of architecture, and symbolic emblems, most expressive, are selected by the fraternity to imprint on the mind wise and serious truth; and thus, through a succession of ages, are transmitted, unimpaired, most excellent tenets of our institution." Here ends the work part of the Fellow Craft degree. It will be observed that the candidate has received, in this place, the second section of the lecture on this degree. This course is not generally pursued, but it is much the most instructive method, and when it is omitted I generally conclude that it is for want of a knowledge of the lecture. Monitorial writers [who are by no means coeval with Masonry] all write and copy very much after each other, and they all inserted in their books all those clauses of the several lectures which are not considered by the wise ones as tending to develop the secrets of Masonry. In some instances they change the phraseology a little; in others, they are literal extracts from the lectures. This, it is said, is done to facilitate the progress of learners or young Masons when in fact it has the contrary effect. All lecture teachers (and there are many traveling about the country with recommendations from some of their distinguished brethren) when they come to any of those clauses, will say to their pupils: "I have not committed that; it is in the Monitor; you can learn it at your leisure." This course of procedure subjects the learner to the necessity of making his own questions, and, of course, answering monitorially, whether the extracts from the lectures are literal or not. Again, there is not a perfect sameness in all the Monitors, or they could not all get copyrights; hence the great diversity in the lectures as well as the work. The following charge is, or ought to be, delivered to the candidate after he has got through the ceremonies; but he is generally told, "It is in the Monitor, and you can read it at your leisure."

"Brother, being advanced to the second degree of Masonry, we congratulate you on your preferment. The internal and not the external qualifications of a man are what Masonry regards. As you increase in knowledge, you will improve in social intercourse. It is unnecessary to recapitulate the duties which, as a Mason, you are bound to discharge, or enlarge on the necessity of a strict adherence to them as your own experience must have established their value. Our laws and regulations you are strenuously to support and be always ready to assist in seeing them duly executed. You are not to palliate or aggravate the offences of your brethren, but in the decision of every trespass against our rules you are to judge with candor, admonish with friendship, and reprehend with justice. The study of the liberal arts, that valuable branch of education, which tends so effectually to polish and adorn the mind, is earnestly recommended to your consideration; especially the science of geometry, which is established as the basis of our art. Geometry or Masonry, originally synonymous terms, being of a divine moral nature, is enriched with the most useful knowledge; while it proves the wonderful properties of nature, it demonstrates the more important truths of morality. Your past behavior and regular deportment have merited the honor which we have now conferred; and in your new character it is expected that you will conform to the principles of the order by steadily persevering in the practice of every commendable virture. Such is the nature of your engagements as a Fellow Craft, and to these duties you are bound by the most sacred ties."

I will now proceed with the lecture on this degree. It is divided into two sections.

## SECTION FIRST.

"Are you a Fellow Craft Mason?"

Ans. "I am—try me."

"By what will you be tried?"

Ans. "By the square."

"Why by the square?"

Ans. "Because it is an emblem of virtue."

"What is a square?"

Ans. "An angle extending to ninety degrees, or the fourth part of a circle."

"Where were you prepared to be made a Fellow Craft Mason?"

Ans. "In a room adjacent to the body of a just and lawfully constituted lodge of such, duly assembled in a room or place, representing the middle chamber of King Solomon's temple."

"How were you prepared?"

Ans. "By being divested of all metals; neither naked nor clothed; barefoot nor shod; hood-winked; with a cable-tow twice round my neck; in which situation I was conducted to the door of the lodge, where I gave two distinct knocks."

What did those two distinct knocks allude to?"

Ans. "The second degree in Masonry, it being that on which I was about to enter."

"What was said to you from within?"

Ans. 'Who comes there? Who comes there?"

"Your answer?"

Ans. "A worthy brother who has been regularly initiated as an Entered Apprentice Mason, served a proper time as such, and now wishes for further light in Masonry by being passed to the degree of a Fellow Craft."

"What was then said to you from within?"

Ans. "I was asked if it was of my own free will and

accord I made this request; if I was duly and truly prepared worthy, and well qualified, and had made suitable proficiency in the preceding degree; all of which being answered in the affirmative, I was asked by what further rights I expected to obtain so great a benefit."

"Your answer?"

Ans. "By the benefit of a pass-word."

"What is that pass-word?"

Ans. "Shibboleth."

"What further was said to you from within?"

Ans. "I was bid to wait till the Worshipful Master in the east was made acquainted with my request, and his answer returned."

"After his answer was returned what followed?"

Ans. "I was caused to enter the lodge."

"How did you enter?"

Ans. "On the angle of the square, presented to my naked right breast, in the name of the Lord."

"How were you then disposed of?"

Ans. "I was conducted twice regularly round the lodge and halted at the Junior Warden in the south, where the same questions were asked and answers returned as at the door.

"How did the Junior Warden dispose of you?"

Ans. "He ordered me to be conducted to the Worshipful Master in the east, where the same questions were asked and answers returned as before, who likewise demanded of me from whence I came and whither I was traveling."

"Your answer?"

Ans. "From the west, and traveling to the east."

"Why did you leave the west and travel to the east?"

Ans. "In search of more light."

"How did the Worshipful then dispose of you?'

Ans. "He ordered me to be be conducted back to the west, from whence I came, and put in care of the Senior Warden, who taught me how to approach the east. by advancing upon two upright regular steps to the second step, my feet forming the right angle of an oblong square, and my body erect at the altar before the Worshipful Master.

"What did the Worshipful Master do with you?"

Ans. "He made a Fellow Craft Mason of me."

"How?"

Ans. "In due form."

"What was that due form?"

Ans. "My right knee bare, bent, my left knee forming a square, my right hand on the Holy Bible, Square and Compass, my left arm forming an angle supported by the Square, and my hand in a vertical position, in which posture I took upon me the solemn oath or obligation of a Fellow Craft Mason." [See page 52 for obligation.]

"After your oath of obligation what was said to you?"

Ans. "I was asked what I most desired."

"Your answer?"

Ans. "More light."

"On being brought to light, what did you discover different from before?"

Ans. "One point of the Compass elevated above the Square, which denoted light in this degree, but as one point was yet in obscurity, it was to remind me that I was yet one material point in the dark respecting Masonry."

"What did you next discover?"

Ans. "The Worshipful Master approaching me from the east, under the sign and due-guard of a Fellow Craft Mason, who presented me with his right hand, in token of brotherly love and confidence, and proceeded to give me the pass-grip and word of a Fellow Craft Mason, and bid me rise and salute the Junior and Senior Wardens, and convince them that I had been regularly passed to the degree of a Fellow Craft, and had the sign, grip, and word of a Fellow Craft Mason."

"What did you next discover?"

Ans. "The Worshipful Master approaching me a second time from the east, who presented me with a lambskin or white apron, which he said he hoped I would continue to wear with honor to myself, and satisfaction and advantage to the brethren."

"What were you next presented with?"

Ans. "The working tools of a Fellow Craft Mason."

"What are they?"

Ans. "The Plumb, Square, and Level.

"What do they teach?" [I think this question ought to be "How explained?"]

Ans. "The Plumb is an instrument made use of by operative Masons to raise perpendiculars, the Square to square their work, and the Level to lay horizontals; but we, as Free and Accepted Masons, are taught to make use of them for more noble and glorious purposes: The Plumb admonishes us to walk uprightly in our several stations before God and man, squaring our actions by the square of virtue, and remembering that we are all traveling upon the level of time to that undiscovered country from whose bourne no traveler returns."

"What were you next presented with?"

Ans. "Three precious jewels."

"What were they?"

Ans. "Faith, hope, and charity."

"What do they teach?"

Ans. "Faith in God, hope in immortality, and charity to all mankind."

"How were you then disposed of?"

Ans. "I was conducted out of the lodge, and invested of what I had been divested."

## SECTION SECOND.

"Have you ever worked as a Fellow Craft Mason?"

Ans. "I have in speculative; but our forefathers wrought both in speculative and operative Masonry."

"Where did they work?"

Ans. "At the building of King Solomon's temple, and many other Masonic edifices."

"How long did they work?"

Ans. "Six days."

"Did they not work on the seventh?"

Ans. "They did not."

"Why so?"

Ans. "Because in six days God created the heavens and

the earth, and rested on the seventh day; the seventh day, therefore, our ancient brethren consecrated as a day of rest from their labors; thereby enjoying more frequent opportunities to contemplate the glorious works of creation, and adore their great Creator."

"Did you ever return to the sanctum sanctorum, or holy of holies, of King Solomon's temple?"

Ans. "I did."

"By what way?"

Ans. "Through a long porch or alley."

"Did anything particular strike your attention on your return?"

Ans. "There did, viz.: two large columns, or pillars, one on the left hand and the other on the right."

"What was the name of the one on your left hand?"

Ans. "Boaz, to denote strength."

"What was the name of the one on your right hand?"

Ans. "Jachin, denoting establishment."

"What do they collectively allude to?"

Ans. "A passage in Scripture wherein God has declared in his word, 'In strength shall this house be established.'"

"What were their dimensions?"

Ans. "Eighteen cubits in height, twelve in circumference, and four in diameter."

"Were they adorned with anything?"

Ans. "They were, with two large Chapiters, one on each."

"Were they ornamented with anything?"

Ans. "They were, with wreaths of net-work, lily-work, and pomegranates."

"What do they denote?"

Ans. "Unity, peace, and plenty."

"Why so?"

Ans. "Net-work, from its connection, denotes union; lily-work, from its whiteness and purity, denotes peace; and pomegranates from the exuberance of its seed, denotes plenty."

"Were those columns adorned with anything further?"

Ans. "They were, viz.: two large globes or balls, one on each."

"Did they contain anything?"

Ans. "They did, viz.: All the maps and charts of the celestial and terrestrial bodies."

"Why are they said to be so extensive?"

Ans "To denote the universality of Masonry, and that a Mason's charity ought to be equally extensive."

"What was their composition?"

Ans. "Molten or cast brass."

"Who cast them?"

Ans "Our Grand Master, Hiram Abiff."

"Where were they cast?"

Ans. "On the banks of the river Jordan, in the clay ground between Succoth and Zaradatha, where King Solomon ordered these and all other holy vessels to be cast."

"Were they cast sound or hollow?"

Ans. "Hollow."

"What was their thickness?"

Ans. "Four inches or a hand-breadth."

"Why were they cast hollow?"

Ans. "The better to withstand inundations and conflagrations; were the archives of Masonry and contained the constitution, rolls and records."

"What did you next come to?"

Ans. "A long, winding stair-case, with three, five, seven steps or more."

"What do the three steps allude to?"

Ans. "The three principal supports in Masonry, viz.: wisdom, strength and beauty."

"What do the five steps allude to?"

Ans. "The five orders in architecture, and the five human senses."

"What are the five orders in architecture?"

Ans. "The Tuscan, Doric, Ionic, Corinthian and Composite."

"What are the five human senses?"

Ans. "Hearing, seeing, feeling, smelling and tasting, the first three of which have ever been deemed highly essential among Masons: hearing, to hear the word; seeing, to see the sign, and feeling, to feel the grip, whereby one Mason may know another in the dark as well as the light.

"What do the seven steps allude to?"

Ans. "The seven sabbatical years, seven years of famine, seven years in building the Temple, seven golden candlesticks, seven wonders of the world, seven planets; but more especially the seven liberal arts and sciences, which are grammar, rhetoric, logic, arithmetic, geometry, music and astronomy. For these and many other reasons the number seven has ever been held in high estimation among Masons."

"What did you next come to?"

Ans. "The outer door of the middle chamber of King Solomon's Temple, which I found partly open, but closely tyled by the Junior Warden."

"How did you gain admission?"

Ans. "By a pass and token of a pa

"What was the name of the pass?"

Ans. "Shibboleth."

"What does it denote?"

Ans. "Plenty."

"Why so?"

Ans. "From an ear of corn being placed at the water ford."

"Why was this pass instituted?"

Ans. "In consequence of a quarrel which had long existed between Jeptha, judge of Israel, and the Ephraimites; the latter of whom had long been a stubborn rebellious people whom Jeptha had endeavored to subdue by lenient measures, but to no effect. The Ephraimites being highly incensed against Jeptha for not being called to fight and share in the rich spoils of the Ammonitish war, assembled a mighty army and passed over the river Jordan to give Jeptha battle, but, he, being apprised of their approach, called together the men of Israel, and gave them battle, and put them to flight; and, to make his victory more complete, he ordered guards to be placed at the different passes on the banks of the river Jordan, and commanded, if the Ephraimites passed that way, that they should pronounce the word Shibboleth; but they, being of a different tribe, pronounced it Seboleth; which trifling defect proved them spies, and cost them their lives: and there fell that day at the different passes on the banks of the river Jordan, forty and two thousand. This word was also used by our ancient brethren to distinguish a friend from foe, and has since been adopted as a proper pass-word to be given before entering any well regulated and governed lodge of Fellow Craft Masons."

"What did you next come to?"

Ans. "The inner door of the middle chamber of King Solomon's Temple, which I found partly open, but closely tyled by the Senior Warden."

"How did you gain admission?"

Ans. "By the grip and word."

"How did the Senior Warden dispose of you?"

Ans. "He ordered me to be conducted to the Worshipful Master in the east, who informed me that I had been admitted into the middle chamber of King Solomon's Temple, for the sake of the letter G."

"Does it denote anything?"

Ans. "It does. DEITY, before whom we should all bow with reverence, worship and adore. It also denotes geometry, the fifth science; it being that on which this degree was principally founded."

Thus ends the second degree of Masonry.

## THE THIRD, OR MASTER MASON'S DEGREE.

The traditional account of the death and several burials, and resurrection of Hiram Abiff, the widow's son as hereafter narrated], admitted as facts, this degree is certainly very interesting. The Bible informs us that there was a person of that name employed at the building of King Solomon's Temple; but neither the Bible, the writings of Josephus, nor any other writings, however ancient, of which I have any knowledge, furnish any information respecting his death. It certainly is very singular, that a man so celebrated as Hiram Abiff, was an arbiter between Solomon, king of Israel, and Hiram, king of Tyre, universally acknowledged as the third most distinguished man then living, and in many respects the greatest man in the world, should pass off the stage of action in the presence of King Solomon, three thousand three hundred grand overseers, and one hundred and fifty thousand workmen, with whom he had spent a number of years, and neither King Solomon, his bosom friend, nor any other among his numerous friends even recorded his death or anything about him. I make these remarks now, hoping that it may induce some person who has time and capacity to investigate the subject, and promulgate the result of his investigation. I shall let the subject rest where it is, at present; it is not intended that it should form any part of this little volume. The principal object of this work is to lay before the world a true history of Freemasonry, without saying anything for or against it.

A person who has received the two preceding degrees, and wishes to be raised to the sublime degree of a Master Mason, is [the lodge being opened as in the preceding degrees] conducted from the preparation room to the door, [the manner of preparing him is particularly explained in the lecture] where he gives three distinct knocks, when the Senior Warden rises and says, "Worshipful, while we are peaceably at work on the third degree of Masonry, under the influence of humanity, brotherly love, and affection, the door of our lodge appears to be alarmed."

The Master to the Senior Deacon, "Brother Senior, enquire the cause of that alarm."

The Senior Deacon then steps to the door and answers the three knocks that have been given by three more: [these knocks are much louder than those given on any occasion, other than that of the admission of candidates in the several degrees] one knock is then given without and answered by one within, when the door is partly opened and the Junior Deacon asks, "Who comes there? Who comes there? Who comes there?"

The Senior Deacon answers, "A worthy brother who has been regularly initiated as an Entered Apprentice Mason, passed to the degree of a Fellow Craft, and now wishes for further light in Masonry by being raised to the sublime degree of a Master Mason."

Junior Deacon to Senior Deacon, "Is it of his own free will and accord he makes this request?"

Ans. "It is."

Junior Deacon to Senior Deacon, "Is he duly and truly prepared."

Ans. "He is."

Junior Deacon to Senior Deacon, "Is he worthy and well qualified?"

Ans. "He is."

Junior Deacon to Senior Deacon, "Has he made suitable proficiency in the preceding degrees?"

Ans. "He has."

Junior Deacon to Senior Deacon, "By what further rights does he expect to obtain this benefit?"

Ans. "By the benefit of a pass-word."

Junior Deacon to Senior Deacon, "Has he a pass-word?"

Ans. "He has not, but I have got it for him."

The Junior Deacon to the Senior Deacon, "Will you give it to me?"

The Senior Deacon then whispers in the ear of the Junior Deacon, "TUBAL CAIN."

Junior Deacon says, "The pass is right. Since this is the case, you will wait till the Worshipful Master be made acquainted with his request and his answer returned."

The Junior Deacon then repairs to the Master and gives three knocks as at the door; after answering of which, the same questions are asked and answers returned as at the door, when the Master says, "Since he comes endued with all these necessary qualifications, let him enter this worshipful lodge, in the name of the Lord, and take heed on what he enters."

The Junior Deacon returns to the door and says, "Let

him enter this worshipful lodge, in the name of the Lord, and take heed on what he enters."

In entering, both points of the compass are pressed against his naked right and left breasts, when the Junior Deacon stops the candidate and says, "Brother, when you first entered this lodge, you were received on the point of the compass, pressing your naked left breast, which was then explained to you; when you entered it the second time you were received on the angle of the square, which was also explained to you; on entering now you are received on the two extreme points of the compass, pressing your right and left breasts, which are thus explained: As the most vital parts of man are contained between the two breasts, so are the most valuable tenets of Masonry contained between the two extreme points of the compass, which are virtue, morality, and brotherly love."

The Senior Deacon then conducts the candidate three times regularly round the lodge. [I wish the reader to observe, that on this, as well as every other degree, that the Junior Warden is the first of the three principal officers that the candidate passes, traveling with the sun when he starts round the lodge, and that as he passes the Junior Warden, Senior Warden and Master, the first time going round, they each give one rap, the second time two raps, and third time three raps each. The number of raps given on those occasions are the same as the number of the degree, except the first degree, on which three are given, I always thought improperly.] During the time the candidate is traveling round the room, the Master reads the following passages of Scripture, the conductor and candidate traveling and the Master reading so that the traveling and reading terminate at the same time:

"Remember now thy Creator in the days of thy youth, while the evil days come not, nor the years draw nigh when thou shalt say, I have no pleasure in them while the sun or the light, or the moon, or the stars be not darkened, nor the clouds return after the rain; in the day when the keepers of the house shall tremble, and the strong men shall bow themselves, and the grinders shall cease because they are few, and those that look out of the windows be darkened, and the doors shall be shut in the streets; when the sound of the grinding is low, and he shall rise up at the voice of the bird, and all the daughters of music shall be brought low. Also, when they shall be afraid of that which is high, and fears shall be in the way, and the almond tree shall flourish, and the grasshopper shall be a burden, and desire shall fail; because man goeth to his long home, and the mourners go about the streets; 'or ever the silver cord be loosed, or the golden bowl be broken, or the pitcher be broken at the fountain, or the wheel at the cistern. Then shall the dust return to the earth as it was; and the spirit shall return unto God who gave it."

The conductor and candidate halt at the Junior Warden in the South, where the same questions are asked and answers returned as at the door. He is then conducted to the Senior Warden in the west, where the same questions are asked and answers returned as before; from whence he is conducted to the Worshipful Master in the east, who asks the same questions and receives the same answers as before, and who likewise asks the candidate from whence he came. and whither he is traveling.

Ans. "From the west, and traveling to the east."

"Why do you leave the west, and travel to the east?"

Ans. "In search of more light."

The Master then says to the Senior Deacon, "You will please conduct him back to the west, from whence he came and put him in care of the Senior Warden, and request him to teach the candidate how to approach the east, by advancing upon three upright, regular steps to the third step, his feet forming a square, his body erect at the altar, before the Worshipful Master, and place him in a proper position to take upon him the solemn oath or obligation of a Master Mason."

The Master then comes to the candidate and says, "Brother, you are now placed in a proper position [the lecture explains it] to take upon you the solemn oath or obligation of a Master Mason, which I assure you, as before, is neither to affect your religion or politics. If you are willing to take it, repeat your name and say after me:"

I, A. B., of my own free will and accord, in the presence

of Almighty God, and this worshipful lodge of Master Masons, dedicated to God, and held forth to the holy order of St. John, do hereby and hereon most solemnly and sincerely promise and swear, in addition to my former obligations, that I will not give the degree of a Master Mason to any of an inferior degree, nor to any other being in the known world, except it be to a true and lawful brother or brethren Master Masons, within the body of a just and lawfully constituted lodge of such; and not unto him nor unto them whom I shall hear so to be, but unto him and them only whom I shall find so to be, after strict trial and due examination, or lawful information received. Furthermore do I promise and swear, that I will not give the Master's word which I shall hereafter receive, neither in the lodge nor out of it, except it be on the five points of fellowship, and then not above my breath. Furthermore do I promise and swear, that I will not give the grand hailing sign of distress except I am in real distress, or for the benefit of the Craft when at work; and should I ever see that sign given or the word accompanying it, and the person who gave it appearing to be in distress I will fly to his relief at the risk of my life, should there be a greater probability of saving his life than losing my own. Furthermore do I promise and swear that I will not wrong this lodge, nor a brother of this degree to the value of one cent, knowingly, myself, or suffer it to be done by others, if in my power to prevent it. Furthermore do I promise and swear, that I will not be at the initiating, passing and raising a candidate at one communication, without a regular dispensation from the Grand Lodge for the same.

Furthermore do I promise and swear that I will not be at the initiating, passing, or raising a candidate in a clandestine lodge, I knowing it to be such. Furthermore do I promise and swear that I will not be at the initiating of an old man in dotage, a young man in nonage, an Atheist, irreligious libertine, idiot, mad-man, hermaphrodite, or woman. Furthermore do I promise and swear that I will not speak evil of a brother Master Mason, neither behind his back nor before his face, but will apprise him of all approaching danger, if in my power. Furthermore do I promise and swear that I will not violate the chastity of a Master Mason's wife, mother, sister, or daughter, I knowing them to be such, nor suffer it to be done by others, if in my power to prevent it.

Furthermore do I promise and swear that I will support the constitution of the Grand Lodge of the state of ——, under which the lodge is held, and conform to all the by-laws, rules, and regulations of this or any other lodge of which I may at any time hereafter become a member.

Furthermore do I promise and swear that I will obey all regular signs, summonses, or tokens given, handed, sent, or thrown to me from the hand of a brother Master Mason, or from the body of a just and lawfully constituted lodge of such, provided it be within the length of my cable-tow.

Furthermore do I promise and swear that a Master Mason's secrets, given to me in charge as such, and I knowing them to be such, shall remain as secure and inviolable in my breast as in his own, when communicated to me, murder and treason excepted; and they left to my own election.

Furthermore do I promise and swear that I will go on a Master Mason's errand whenever required, even should I have to go bare-foot and bare-headed, if within the length of my cable-tow.

Furthermore do I promise and swear that I will always remember a brother Master Mason when on my knees offering up my devotions to Almighty God.

Furthermore do I promise and swear that I will be aiding and assisting all poor, indigent Master Masons, their wives and orphans, wheresoever disposed around the globe, as far as in my power, without injuring myself or family materially.

Furthermore do I promise and swear that if any part of my solemn oath or obligation be omitted at this time, that I will hold myself amenable thereto whenever informed. To all which I do most sincerely promise and swear, with a fixed and steady purpose of mind in me to keep and perform the same, binding myself under no less penalty than to have my body severed in two in the midst, and divided to the north and south, my bowels burnt to ashes in the center, and the ashes scattered before the four winds of heaven, that there might not the least track or trace of remembrance remain among men. or Masons, of so vile and perjured a wretch as ⁘

should be, were I ever to prove willfully guilty of violating any part of this my solemn oath or obligation of a Master Mason. So help me God, and keep me steadfast in the due performance of the same.

The Master then asks the candidate, "What do you most desire?"

The candidate answers after his prompter, "More light."

The bandage which was tied round his head in the preparation room is, by one of the brethren who stands behind him for that purpose, loosened and put over both eyes, and he is immediately brought to light in the same manner as in the preceding degree, except three stamps on the floor and three claps of the hands are given in this degree. On being brought to light, the Master says to the candidate, "You first discover, as before, three great lights in Masonry, by the assistance of three lesser, with this difference: both points of the compass are elevated above the square, which denotes to you that you are about to receive all the light that can be conferred on you in a Master's lodge." The Master steps back from the candidate and says, "Brother, you now discover me, as Master of this lodge, approaching you from the east, under the sign and due-guard of a Master Mason. "The

Grand Hailing Sign of Distress.

sign is given by raising both hands and arms to the elbows, perpendicularly, one on each side of the head, the elbows forming a square. The words accompanying this sign, in case of distress, are, "O Lord, my God! is there no help for the widow's son?" As the last words drop from your lips, you let your hands fall, in that manner best calculated to indicate solemnity. King Solomon is said to have made this exclamation on the receipt of the information of the death of Hiram Abiff. Masons are all charged never to give the words except in the dark, when the sign cannot be seen.

Here Masons differ very much; some contend that Solomon gave this sign and made this exclamation when in-

½Note.—The sign as now given is shown on the next page.

formed of Hiram's death, and work accordingly in their lodges. Others say the sign was given and the exclamation made at the grave, when Solomon went to raise Hiram, and, of course, they work accordingly; that is to say, the Master who governs the lodge, holding the latter opinion, gives the sign, etc., at the grave, when he goes to raise the body, and vice versa.

The Due Guard is made by holding both hands in front, palms down, as shown in cut, and alludes to the manner of holding the hands while taking the obligation of Master Mason.

The Penal Sign is given by putting the right hand to the left side of the bowels, the hand open, with the thumb next to the belly, and drawing it across the belly, and letting it fall; this is done tolerably quick. This alludes to the penalty of the obligation: "Having my body severed in twain," etc. See page 75. After the Master has given the sign and due guard, which does not take more than a minute,

Due Guard.  Penal Sign.
Master Mason.

he says, "Brother, I now present you with my right hand, in token of brotherly love and affection, and with it the pass-grip and word."

The pass-grip is given by pressing the thumb between the joints of the second and third fingers where they join the hand; the word or name is TUBAL CAIN. It is the pass-word to the Master's degree. The Master, after giving the candidate the pass-grip and word, bids him rise and salute the Junior and Senior Wardens, and convince them that he is an obligated Master Mason, and is in possession of the pass-grip and word. While the Wardens are examining the candidate, the Master returns to the east and gets an apron, and, as he returns to the candidate, one of the Wardens (sometimes both) says to the Master, "Worshipful, we are satisfied that Bro. ——— is an obligated Master Mason." The Master then says to the candidate, "Brother, I now have the honor to present you with a lamb-skin or white apron, as before, which I hope you will continue to wear, with credit to yourself and satisfaction and advantage to the brethren; you will please carry it to the Senior Warden in the west, who will teach you how to wear it as a Master Mason."

The Senior Warden ties on the apron and lets the flaps

fall down before, in its natural and common situation.

The Master returns to the seat and the candidate is conducted to him. Master to candidate, "Brother, I perceive you are dressed, it is of course necessary you should have tools to work with. I will now present you with the working tools of the Master Mason, and explain their use to you. The working tools of a Master Mason are all the implements of Masonry indiscriminately, but more especially the trowel. The trowel is an instrument made use of by operative masons to spread the cement which unites a building into one mass, but we, as Free and Accepted Masons, are taught to make use of it for the more noble and glorious purpose of spreading the cement of brotherly love and affection; that cement which unites us into one sacred band or society of friends and brothers, among whom no contention should ever exist but that noble contention, or, rather, emulation, of who can best work or best agree. I also present you with three precious jewels; their names are *Humanity, Friendship,* and *Brotherly Love.*

Brother, you are not invested with all the secrets of this degree, nor do I know whether you ever will be until I know how you withstand the amazing trials and dangers that await you.

You are now about to travel, to give us a specimen of your fortitude, perseverance, and fidelity in the preservation of what you have already received. Fare you well, and may the Lord be with you and support you through all your trials and difficulties." [In some lodges they make him pray before he starts.] The candidate is then conducted out of the lodge, clothed, and returns; as he enters the door his conductor says to him, "Brother, we are now in a place representing the sanctum sanctorum, or holy of holies, of King Solomon's temple. It was the custom of our Grand Master, Hiram Abiff, every day at high twelve, when the Crafts were from labor to refreshment, to enter into the sanctum sanctorum, and offer up his devotions to the ever living God. Let us, in imitation of him, kneel and pray." They then kneel and the conductor says the following prayer:

"Thou, O God, knowest our down-sitting and up-rising, and understandest our thoughts afar off, shield and defend us from the evil intentions of our enemies, and support us under the trials and afflictions which we are destined to endure while traveling through this vale of tears. Man that is born of a woman is of few days and full of trouble. He cometh forth as a flower, and is cut down, he fleeth also as a shadow, and continueth not. Seeing his days are determined, the number of months are with thee, thou hast appointed his bounds that he cannot pass; turn from him that he may rest, till he shall accomplish his day. For there is hope of a tree, if it be cut down, that it will sprout again, and that the tender branch thereof will not cease. But man dieth and wasteth away; yea, man giveth up the ghost, and where is he? As the waters fall from the sea, and the flood decayeth and drieth up, so man lieth down and riseth not up till the heavens shall be no more. Yet, O Lord, have compassion on the children of thy creation; administer unto them comfort in time of trouble, and save them with an everlasting salvation. Amen, so mote it be."

They then rise, and the conductor says to the candidate: "Brother, in further imitation of our Grand Master, Hiram Abiff, let us retire at the south gate." They then advance to the Junior Warden [who represents *Jubela*, one of the ruffians], who exclaims, "Who comes here?" [The room is dark, or the candidate hoodwinked.] The conductor answers, "Grand Master, Hiram Abiff."

"Our Grand Master, Hiram Abiff!" exclaims the ruffian; "he is the very man I wanted to see." [Seizing the candidate by the throat at the same time, and jerking him about with violence.] 'Give me the Master Mason's word or I'll take your life!" The conductor replies, "I cannot give it now, but if you will wait till the Grand Lodge assembles at Jerusalem, if you are found worthy, you shall then receive it, otherwise you cannot." The ruffian then gives the candidate a blow with the twenty-four inch gauge across the throat, on which he fled to the west gate, where he was accosted by the second ruffian, *Jubelo*, with more violence, and on his refusal to comply with his request, he gave him a severe blow with the square across his breast, on which he attempted to make his escape at the east gate, where he was accosted by the third ruffian, *Jubelum*, with still more violence, and on refusing to comply with his request, the ruffian gave him a violent blow with the common gavel on the forehead, which brought him

to the floor; on which one of them exclaimed, "What shall we do? We have killed our Grand Master, Hiram Abiff!"

Another answers, "Let us carry him out of the east gate, and bury him in the rubbish till low twelve, and then meet and carry him a westerly course and bury him."

The candidate is taken up in a blanket, on which he fell, and carried to the west end of the lodge, and covered up and left; by this time the Master has resumed his seat [King Solomon is supposed to arrive at the temple at this juncture] and calls to order, and asks the Senior Warden the cause of all that confusion.

The Senior Warden answers, "Our Grand Master, Hiram Abiff, is missing, and there are no plans or designs laid down on the Trestle-board for the Craft to pursue their labors."

The Master, alias King Solomon, replies, "Our Grand Master missing! Our Grand Master has always been very punctual in his attendance; I fear he is indisposed; assemble the Crafts, and search in and about the temple, and see if he can be found.

They all shuffle about the floor awhile, when the Master calls them to order and asks the Senior Warden, "What success?" He answers, "We cannot find our Grand Master, my lord."

The Master then orders the Secretary to call the roll of workmen and see whether any of them are missing.

The Secretary calls the roll and says, "I have called the roll, my lord, and find that there are three missing, viz.: Jubela, Jubelo, and Jubelum."

His lordship then observed, "This brings to my mind a circumstance that took place this morning. Twelve Fellow Crafts, clothed in white gloves and aprons, in token of their innocence, came to me and confessed that they twelve, with three others, had conspired to extort the Master Mason's word from their Grand Master, Hiram Abiff, and in case of refusal to take his life. They twelve had recanted, but feared the other three had been base enough to carry their atrocious designs into execution."

Solomon then ordered twelve Fellow Crafts to be drawn from the bands of the workmen, clothed in white gloves and aprons, in token of their innocence, and sent three east, three west, three north, and three south in search of the ruffians, and if found to fetch them forward.

Here the members all shuffle about the floor awhile, and fall in with a reputed traveler, and inquire of him if he had seen any traveling men that way; he tells them that he has seen three that morning near the coast of Joppa. who from their dress and appearance were Jews, and who were workmen from the temple, inquiring for a passage to Ethiopia, but were unable to obtain one in consequence of an embargo which had recently been laid on all the shipping, and had turned back into the country.

The Master now calls them to order again, and asks the Senior Warden, "What success?" He answers by relating what had taken place.

Solomon observes, "I had this embargo laid to prevent the ruffians from making their escape," and adds, "You will go and search again, and search till you find them, if possible, and if they are not found the twelve who confessed shall be considered as the reputed murderers and suffer accordingly."

The members all start again and shuffle about awhile.

until one of them, as if by accident, finds the body of Hiram Abiff, alias the candidate, and hails his traveling companions, who join him, and while they are hammering out something over the candidate the three reputed ruffians, who are seated in a private corner near the candidate, are heard to exclaim in the following manner:

First, Jubela—"O that my throat had been cut across, my tongue torn out, and my body buried in the rough sands of the sea, at low water mark, where the tide ebbs and flows twice in twenty-four hours, ere I had been accessory to the death of so good a man as our Grand Master, Hiram Abiff!"

The second, Jubelo—"O that my left breast had been torn open and my heart and vitals taken from thence and thrown over my left shoulder, carried into the valley of Jehosaphat, and there to become a prey to the wild beasts of the field and vultures of the air, ere I had conspired the death of so good a man as our Grand Master, Hiram Abiff!"

The third, Jubelum—"O that my body had been severed in two in the midst, and divided to the north and south, my bowels burnt to ashes in the center, and the ashes scattered by the four winds of heaven, that there might not the least track or remembrance remain among men, or Masons, of so vile and perjured a wretch as I am; ah, Jubela and Jubelo, it was I that struck him harder than you both. It was I that gave him the fatal blow; it was I that killed him outright;"

The three Fellow Crafts who had stood by the candidate all this time, listening to the ruffians, whose voices they recognized, say, one to the other:

"What shall we do; there are three of them, and only three of us?"

"It is," said one, in reply; "our cause is good, let us seize them."

On which they rush forward, seize and carry them to the Master, to whom they relate what had passed. The Master then addresses them in the following manner [they in many lodges kneel or lie down, in token of their guilt and penitence]:

"Well, Jubela, what have you got to say to yourself, guilty or not guilty?"

Ans. "Guilty, my lord."
"Jubelo, guilty or not guilty?"
Ans. "Guilty, my lord."
"Jubelum, guilty or not guilty?"
Ans. "Guilty, my lord."
The Master, to the three Fellow Crafts who took them:

"Take them without the west gate of the temple and have them executed according to the several imprecations of their own mouths."

They are then hurried off to the west end of the room. Here this part of the farce ends. The Master then orders fifteen Fellow Crafts to be selected from the bands of workmen, and sent, three east, three west, three north, three south, and three in and about the temple, in search of their Grand Master, Hiram Abiff [in some lodges they send only twelve, when their own lectures say fifteen were sent], and charges them, if they find the body, to examine carefully on and about it for the Master's word or a key to it. The three that travel a westerly course come to the candidate, and finger about him a little, and are called to order by the Master, when they report that they had found the grave of their Grand Master, Hiram Abiff, and, on moving the earth till they come to the body, they involuntarily found their hands raised in this position (showing it at the same time; it is the due-guard of this degree), to guard their nostrils against the offensive effluvia which arose from the grave, and that they had searched carefully on and about the body for the Master's word, but had not discovered anything but a faint resemblance of the letter G on the left breast. The Master, on the receipt of this information (raising himself), raises his hands three several times above his head (as herein before described) and exclaims, "Nothing but a faint resemblance of the letter G! That is not the Master's word nor a key to it. I fear the Master's word is forever lost! Nothing but a faint resemblance to the letter G! That is not the Master's word nor a key to it. I fear the Master's word is forever lost! [The third acclamation is different from the other two; attend to it. It has been described on page 76.] Nothing but a faint resemblance of the letter G! That is not the Master's word nor a key to it. O Lord, my God, is there no help for the widow's son?"

The Master then orders the Junior Warden to summon a lodge of Entered Apprentice Masons, and repair to the grave and try to raise their Grand Master by the Entered Apprentice's grip. They go to the candidate and take hold of his forefinger and pull it; return and tell the Master that they could not raise him by the Entered Apprentice's grip; that the skin cleaved from the bone. A lodge of Fellow Crafts are then sent, who act as before, except that they pull the candidate's second finger. The Master then directs the Senior Warden (generally) to summon a lodge of Master Masons, and says, "I will go with them myself in person, and try to raise the body by the Master's grip, or lion's paw." [Some say by the strong grip, or lion's paw.] They then all assemble round the candidate, the Master having declared that the first word spoken after the body was raised should be adopted as a substitute for the Master's word, for the government of Master Masons' lodges in all future generations. He proceeds to raise the candidate, *alias* the representative of the dead body of Hiram Abiff. He (the candidate) is raised on what is called the five points of fellowship, which are foot to foot, knee to knee, breast to breast, hand to back and mouth to ear. This is done by putting the inside of your right foot to the inside of the right foot of the person to whom you are going to give the word, the inside of your knee to his, laying your right breast against his, your left hands on the back of each other, and your mouths to each other's right ear (in which position alone you are permitted to give the word), and whisper the word *Mahhah-bone.* The Master's grip is given by taking hold of each other's hand as though you were going to shake hands, and sticking the nails of each of your fingers into the joint of the other's wrist where it unites with the hand. In this position

the candidate is raised, he keeping his whole body stiff, as though dead. The Master, in raising him, is assisted by some of the brethren, who take hold of the candidate by the arms and shoulders; as soon as he is raised to his feet, they step back and the Master whispers the word Mah-hah-bone in his ear, and causes the candidate to repeat it, telling him, at the same time, that he must never give it in any manner other than that in which he receives it. He is also told that Mah-hah-bone signifies marrow in the bone. They then separate, and the Master then makes the following explanation respecting the five points of fellowship:

Master to candidate. "Brother, foot to foot teaches you that you should, whenever asked, go on a brother's errand, if within the length of your cable-tow, even if you should have to go barefoot and bareheaded. Knee to knee, that you should always remember a Master Mason in your devotions to Almighty God. Breast to breast, that you should keep the Master Mason's secrets, when given to you in charge as such, as secure and inviolable in your breast as they were in his own before communicated to you. Hand to back, that you should support a Master Mason behind his back as before his face. Mouth to ear, that you should support his good name as well behind his back as before his face."

After the candidate is through with what is called the work part, the Master addresses him in the following manner:

"Brother, you may suppose, from the manner you have been dealt with to-night, that we have been fooling with you, or that we have treated you different from others; but I assure you that is not the case. You have this night represented one of the greatest men that ever lived in the tragical catastrophe of his death, burial, and resurrection; I mean Hiram Abiff, the widow's son, who was slain by three ruffians at the building of King Solomon's temple, and who, in his inflexibility, integrity, and fortitude, never was surpassed by man. The history of that momentous event is thus related: Masonic tradition informs us that, at the building of King Solomon's temple, fifteen Fellow Crafts, discovering that the temple was almost finished, and not having the Master Mason's word, became very impatient and entered into a horrid conspiracy to extort the Master Mason's word from their

Grand Master, Hiram Abiff, the first time they met him alone, or take his life, that they might pass as Masters in other countries, and receive wages as such · but, before they could accomplish their designs, twelve of them recanted, but the other three were base enough to carry their atrocious designs into execution. Their names were Jubela, Jubelo, and Jubelum. It was the custom of our Grand Master, Hiram Abiff, every day at high twelve, when the Craft were from labor to refreshment, to enter into the sanctum sanctorum and offer up his devotions to the ever-living God, and draw out his plans and designs on the trestle-board, for the Crafts to pursue their labor. On a certain day (not named in any of our traditional accounts) Jubela, Jubelo, and Jubelum placed themselves at the south, west, and east gates of the temple, and Hiram, having finished his devotions and labor, attempted (as was his usual custom) to retire at the south gate, where he was met by Jubela, who demanded of him the Master Mason's word [some say the secrets of a Master Mason], and on his refusal to give it Jubela gave him a violent blow with the twenty-four inch gauge across the throat; on which Hiram fled to the west gate, where he was accosted in the same manner by Jubelo, but with more violence. Hiram told him that he could not give the word then because Solomon, king of Israel, Hiram, king of Tyre, and himself had entered into a solemn league that the word never should be given unless they three were present; but, if he would wait with patience till the Grand Lodge assembled at Jerusalem, if he was then found worthy he should receive it, otherwise he could not. Jubelo replied, in a very peremptory manner: 'If you do not give me the Master's word I'll take your life'; and on Hiram's refusal to give it Jubelo gave him a severe blow with the square across the left breast, on which he fled to the east gate, where he was accosted by Jubelum in the same manner, but with still more violence. Here Hiram reasoned as before; Jubelum told him that he had heard his caviling with Jubela and Jubelo long enough, and that he was still put off, and the temple was almost finished, and he was determined to have the word or take his life. 'I want it so that I may be able to get wages as a Master Mason in any country to which I may go for employ, after the temple is finished, and that I might be able to support my wife and children.' Hiram persisting in his refusal, he gave Hiram a violent blow with the gavel on the forehead, which felled him to the floor and killed him. They took the body and carried it out of the east gate and buried it in the rubbish till low twelve at night (which is 12 o'clock), when the three met, agreeable to appointment, and carried the body a westerly direction, and buried it at the brow of a hill, in a grave dug due east and west, six feet perpendicular, and made their escape. King Solomon, coming up to the temple at low six in the morning (as was his usual custom), found the Crafts all in confusion, and, on inquiring the cause, was informed that their Grand Master, Hiram Abiff, was missing, and there were no plans and designs laid down on the trestle-board for the Crafts to pursue their labor. Solomon ordered immediate search to be made in and about the Temple for him; no discovery being made, he then ordered the Secretary to call the roll of workmen, to see if any were missing; it appearing that there were three, viz: Jubela, Jubelo and Jubelum, Solomon observed:

"This brings to my mind a circumstance that took place this morning. Twelve Fellow Crafts came to me, dressed in white gloves and aprons in token of their innocence, and confessed that they twelve with three others had conspired to extort the Master Mason's word from their Grand Master, Hiram Abiff, and in case of his refusal to take his life; they twelve had recanted, but feared the other three had been base enough to carry their atrocious design into execution."

Solomon immediately ordered twelve Fellow Crafts to be selected from the bands of the workmen, clothed in white gloves and aprons in token of their innocence, and sent three east, three west, three north and three south, in search of the ruffians, and if found to bring them up before him. The three that traveled a westerly course, coming near the coast of Joppa, fell in with a warfaring man, who informed them that he had seen three men pass that way that morning, who, from their appearance and dress, were workmen from the Temple, inquiring for a passage to Ethiopia, but were unable to obtain one in consequence of an embargo which had recently been laid on all the shipping, and had turned back into the country. After making still further and more diligent search, and after making no further discovery, they returned to the Temple and reported to Solomon the result of their pursuit and inquiries. On which Solomon directed them to go and search again, and search until they found their Grand Master, Hiram Abiff, if possible, and if he was not found, the twelve who had confessed should be considered as the murderers and suffer accordingly.

They returned again in pursuit of the ruffians, and one of the three that traveled a westerly course, being more weary than the rest, sat down at the brow of a hill to rest and refresh himself; and in attempting to rise caught hold of a sprig of cassia, which easily gave way and excited his curiosity, and made him suspicious of a deception, on which he hailed his companions, who immediately assembled, and on examination found that the earth had been recently moved; and, on moving the rubbish, discovered the appearance of a grave; and while they were confabulating about what measure to take, they heard voices issuing from a cavern in the clefts of the rocks, on which they immediately repaired to the place, where they heard the voice of Jubela exclaim, "O! that my throat had been cut across, my tongue torn out, and my body buried in the rough sands of the sea at low water-mark, where the tide ebbs and flows twice in twenty-four hours, ere I had been accessory to the death of so good a man as our Grand Master, Hiram Abiff." On which they distinctly heard the voice of Jubelo exclaim, "O! that my breast had been torn open, and my heart and vitals taken from thence and thrown over my left shoulder, to the valley of Jehosaphat, there to become a prey to the wild beasts of the field and vultures of the air, ere I had conspired to take the life of so good a man as our Grand Master, Hiram Abiff. When they more distinctly heard the voice of Jubelum exclaim, "O! that my body had been severed in two in the midst, and divided to the north and the south, my bowels burnt to ashes in the center, and the ashes scattered by the four winds of heaven, that there might not remain the least track or trace of remembrance among men or Masons of so vile and perjured a wretch as I am, who wilfully took the life of so good a man as our Grand Master, Hiram Abiff. Ah! Jubela and Jubelo, it was I that struck him harder than you both! It

was I that gave him the fatal blow! It was I that killed him
outright!" On which they rushed forward, seized, bound,
and carried them up before King Solomon, who, after hearing the testimony of the three Fellow Crafts, and the three
ruffians having plead guilty, ordered them to be taken out at
the west gate of the Temple and executed agreeable to the
several imprecations of their own mouths. King Solomon
then ordered fifteen Fellow Crafts to be selected from the
bands of the workmen, clothed with white gloves and aprons,
in token of their innocence, and sent three east, three west,
three north, three south and three in and about the Temple,
in search of the body of their Grand Master, Hiram Abiff,
and the three that traveled a westerly course found it under
that sprig of cassia, where a worthy brother sat down to rest
and refresh himself; and on removing the earth till they
came to the coffin, they involuntarily found their hands raised,
as herein before described, to guard their nostrils against the
offensive effluvia that arose from the grave. It is also said
that the body had lain there fourteen days, some say fifteen.
The body was raised in the manner herein before described,
carried up to the Temple, and buried as explained in the
closing clauses of the lecture. Not one third part of the
preceding history of this degree is ever given to a candidate.
A few general, desultory, unconnected remarks are made to
him, and he is generally referred to the manner of raising,
and the lecture, for information as to the particulars. Here
follows a charge which ought to be and sometimes is delivered to the candidate after hearing the history of the degree.

*An address to be delivered to the candidate after the history
has been given.*

"Brother, your zeal for the institution of Masonry, the
progress you have made in the mystery, and your conform-
ity to our regulations, have pointed you out as a proper object of our favor and esteem. You are bound by duty, honor
and gratitude to be faithful to your trust, to support the
dignity of your character on every occasion, and to enforce,
by precept and example, obedience to the tenets of the order.
In the character of Master Mason, you are authorized to correct the errors and irregularities of your uninformed breth-

ren, and to guard them against breach of fidelity. To preserve the reputation of the fraternity, unsullied, must be your constant care—and for this purpose it is your province to recommend to your inferiors, obedience and submission; to your equals, courtesy and affability; to your superiors, kindness and condescension. Universal benevolence you are always to inculcate; and by the regularity of your own behavior, afford the best example for the conduct of others less informed. The ancient landmarks of the order, entrusted to your care, you are carefully to preserve; and never suffer them to be infringed, or countenance a deviation from the established usages and customs of the fraternity. Your virtue, honor, and reputation are concerned in supporting with dignity the character you now bear. Let no motive, therefore, make you swerve from your duty, violate your vows, or betray your trust; but be true and faithful, and imitate the example of that celebrated artist whom you this evening represent; thus you will render yourself deserving the honor which we have conferred, and merit the confidence that we have reposed."

Here follows the lecture on this degree, which is divided into three sections.

## SECTION FIRST.

"Are you a Master Mason"

Ans. "I am—try me, prove me—disprove me if you can."

"Where were you prepared to be made a Master Mason?"

Ans. "In a room adjacent to the body of a just and lawfully constituted lodge of such, duly assembled in a room representing the sanctum sanctorum, or holy of holies, of King Solomon's Temple."

"How were you prepared?"

Ans. "By being divested of all metals; neither naked nor clothed; barefoot nor shod; with a cable-tow three times about my naked body; in which posture I was conducted to the door of the lodge, where I gave three distinct knocks."

"What did those three distinct knocks allude to?"

Ans. "To the third degree of Masonry; it being that on

which I was about to enter."

"What was said to you from within?"

Ans. "Who comes there? Who comes there? Who comes there?"

"Your answer?"

Ans. "A worthy brother who has been regularly initiated as an Entered Apprentice Mason, passed to the degree of a Fellow Craft, and now wishes for further light in Masonry, by being raised to the sublime degree of a Master Mason."

"What further was said to you from within?"

Ans. "I was asked if it was of my own free will and accord I made that request; if I was duly and truly prepared; worthy and well qualified, and had made suitable proficiency in the preceding degrees; all of which being answered in the affirmative, I was asked by what further rights I expected to obtain that benefit."

"Your answer?"

Ans. "By the benefit of a pass-word."

"What is that pass-word?"

Ans. *"Tubal Cain."*

"What next was said to you?"

Ans. "I was bid to wait till the Worshipful Master in the east was made acquainted with my request and his answer returned."

"What followed after his answer was returned?"

Ans. "I was caused to enter the lodge on the two extreme points of the compass, pressing my naked right and left breasts, in the name of the Lord."

"How were you then disposed of?"

Ans. "I was conducted three times regularly round the lodge, and halted at the Junior Warden in the south, where the same questions were asked and answers returned as at the door."

"How did the Junior Warden dispose of you?"

Ans. "He ordered me to be conducted to the Senior Warden in the west, where the same questions were asked and answers returned as before."

"How did the Senior Warden dispose of you?"

Ans. "He ordered me to be conducted to the Worshipful Master in the east, where by him the same questions were asked, and answers returned as before, who likewise demanded of me from whence I came, and whither I was traveling."

"Your answer?"

Ans. "From the east and traveling to the west."

"Why do you leave the east, and travel to the west?"

Ans. "In search of light."

"How did the Worshipful Master then dispose of you?"

Ans. "He ordered me to be conducted back to the west, from whence I came, and put in care of the Senior Warden, who taught me how to approach the east, by advancing upon three upright, regular steps to the third step, my feet forming a square and my body erect at the altar before the Worshipful Master."

"What did the Worshipful Master do with you?"

Ans. "He made an obligated Master Mason of me."

"How?"

Ans. "In due form."

"What was that due form?"

Ans. "Both my knees bare bent, they forming a square; both hands on the Holy Bible, Square and Compass; in which posture I took upon me the solemn oath or obligation of a Master Mason."

"After your obligation, what was said to you?"

Ans. "What do you most desire?"

"Your answer?"

Ans. "More light."

[The bandage round the head is now dropped over the eyes.]

"Did you receive light?"

Ans. "I did."

"On being brought to light on this degree, what did you first discover?"

Ans. "Three great lights in Masonry, by the assistance of three lesser, and both points of the compass elevated above the square, which denoted to me that I had received, or was about to receive all the light that could be conferred on me in a Master's Lodge."

"What did you next discover?"

Ans. "The Worshipful Master approaching me from the east, under the sign and due-guard of a Master Mason, who presented me with his right hand in token of brotherly love and confidence, and proceeded to give me the pass-grip and word of a Master Mason, [the word is the name of the pass-grip] and bid me arise and salute the Junior and Senior Wardens and convince them that I was an obligated Master Mason, and had the sign, pass-grip and word. [Tubal Cain.]

"What did you next discover?"

Ans. "The Worshipful Master approaching me the second time from the east, who presented me with a lamb-skin or white apron, which he said he hoped I would continue to wear, with honor to myself, and satisfaction and advantage to the brethren."

"What were you next presented with?"

Ans. "The working tools of a Master Mason."

"What are they?"

Ans. "All the implements of Masonry indiscriminately, but more especially the trowel."

"How explained?"

Ans. "The trowel is an instrument made use of by operative masons to spread the cement which unites a building into one common mass, but we, as Free and Accepted Masons, are taught to make use of it for the more noble and glorious purpose of spreading the cement of brotherly love and affection, that cement which unites us into one sacred band or society of brothers, among whom no contention should ever exist, but that noble emulation of who can best work or best agree."

"What were you next presented with?"

Ans. "Three precious jewels."

"What are they?"

Ans. "Humanity, friendship and brotherly love."

"How were you then disposed of?"

Ans. "I was conducted out of the lodge and invested with what I had been divested, and returned again in due season."


SECTION SECOND.

"Did you ever return to the sanctum sanctorum or holy of holies of King Solomon's Temple?"

Ans. "I did."

"Was there anything particular took place on your return?"

Ans "There was, viz.: I was accosted by three ruffians, who demanded of me the Master Mason's word."

"Did you give it to them?"

Ans. "I did not, but bid them wait with time and patience till the Grand Lodge assembled at Jerusalem; and then, if they were found worthy, they should receive it; otherwise they could not."

"In what manner were you accosted?"

Ans. "In attempting to retire to the south gate, I was accosted by one of them, who demanded of me the Master Mason's word, and on refusing to comply with his request he gave me a blow with the twenty-four inch gauge, across my breast, on which I fled to the west gate, where I was accosted by the second, with more violence, and on my refusing to comply with his request he gave me a severe blow with the square, across my breast, on which I attempted to make my escape at the east gate, where I was accosted by the third, with still more violence, and on my refusing to comply with his request he gave me a violent blow with the common gavel on the forehead, and brought me to the floor."

"Whom did you represent at that time?"

Ans. "Our Grand Master, Hiram Abiff, who was slain at the building of King Solomon's Temple."

"Was his death premeditated?"

Ans. "It was, by fifteen Fellow Crafts, who conspired to extort from him the Master Mason's word; twelve of whom recanted, but the other three were base enough to carry their atrocious designs into execution."

"What did they do with the body?"

Ans. "They carried it out at the east gate of the Temple and buried it till low twelve at night, when they three met, agreeable to appointment, and carried it a westerly course from the Temple, and buried it under the brow of a hill in a grave six feet due east and west, six feet perpendicular, and made their escape."

"What time was he slain?"

Ans. "At high twelve at noon, when the Crafts were from labor to refreshment."

"How come he to be alone at this time?"

Ans. "Because it was the usual custom of our Grand Master, Hiram Abiff, every day at high twelve, when the

Crafts were from labor to refreshment, to enter into the sanctum sanctorum or holy of holies, and offer up his adorations to the ever living God, and draw out his plans and designs on his trestle-board, for the Crafts to pursue their labor."

"At what time was he missing?"

Ans. "At low six in the morning, when King Solomon came up to the Temple, as usual, to view the work, and found the Crafts all in confusion, and on inquiring the cause, he was informed that their Grand Master, Hiram Abiff, was missing, and no plans or designs were laid down on the trestle-board for the Crafts to pursue their labor."

"What observations did King Solomon make at that time?"

Ans. "He observed that our Grand Master, Hiram Abiff, had always been very punctual in attending, and feared that he was indisposed, and ordered search to be made in and about the Temple, to see if he could be found."

"Search being made and he not found, what further remarks did King Solomon make?"

Ans. "He observed he feared some fatal accident had befallen our Grand Master, Hiram Abiff; that morning twelve Fellow Crafts, clothed in white gloves and aprons in token of their innocence, had confessed that they twelve, with three others, had conspired to extort the Master Mason's word from their Grand Master, Hiram Abiff, or take his life; that they twelve had recanted, but feared the other three had been base enough to carry their atrocious designs into execution."

"What followed?"

Ans. "King Solomon ordered the roll of workmen to be called to see if there were any missing."

"The roll being called, were there any missing?"

Ans. "There were three, viz.: Jubela, Jubelo, Jubelum."

"Were the ruffians ever found?"

Ans. "They were."

"How?"

Ans. "By the wisdom of King Solomon, who ordered twelve Fellow Crafts to be selected from the band of the workmen, clothed in white gloves and aprons in token of their innocence, and sent three east, three west, three north and three sout'n in search of the ruffians, and if **found to** bring them forward."

"What success?"

Ans. "The three that traveled a westerly course from the Temple, coming near the coast of Joppa, were informed by a way-faring man that the three men had been seen that way that morning, who from their appearance and dress were workmen from the Temple, inquiring for a passage to Ethiopia, but were unable to obtain one in consequence of an embargo, which had recently been laid on all the shipping, and had turned back into the country."

"What followed?"

Ans. "King Solomon ordered them to go and search again, and search till they were found, if possible, and if they were not found, that the twelve who had confessed should be considered as the reputed murderers, and suffer accordingly."

"What success?"

Ans. "Cne of the three that traveled a westerly course, from the Temple, being more weary than the rest, sat down under the brow of a hill to rest and refresh himself, and in attempting to rise caught hold of a sprig of cassia, which easily gave way, and excited his curiosity and made him suspicious of a deception, on which he hailed his companions who immediately assembled, and on examination found that the earth had recently been moved, and on moving the rubbish discovered the appearance of a grave; and while they were confabulating about what measures to take, they heard voices issuing from a cavern in the clefts of the rocks; on which they immediately repaired to the place, where they heard the voice of Jubeia exclaim, 'O that my throat had been cut across, my tongue torn out, and my body buried in the rough sands of the sea, at low watermark, where the tide ebbs and flows twice in twenty-four hours, ere I had been accessary to the death of so good a man as our Grand Master, Hiram Abiff!' On which they distinctly heard the voice of Jubelo, 'O that my left breast had been torn open, and my heart and vitals taken from thence and thrown over my left shoulder, carried into the valley of Jehosaphat, and there to become a prey to the wild beasts or the field, and vultures of the air, ere I had conspired the death of so good a man as our Grand Master, Hiram Abiff!'

The third, Jubelum, 'O that my body had been severed in two in the midst, and divided to the north and south, my bowels burnt to ashes in the centre, and the ashes scattered by the four winds of heaven, that there might not the least track or remembrance remain among men or Masons of so vile and perjured a wretch as I am; ah! Jubela, and Jubelo, it was I that struck him harder than you both—it was I that gave him the fatal blow—it was I that killed him outright!'

On which they rushed forward, seized, bound and carried them up to the Temple of King Solomon.

"What did King Solomon do with them?"

Ans. "He ordered them to be executed agreeably to the several imprecations of their own mouths."

"Was the body of our Grand Master, Hiram Abiff, ever found?"

Ans. "It was."

"How?"

Ans. "By the wisdom of King Solomon, who ordered fifteen (in some lodges they say twelve) Fellow Crafts to be selected from the bands of the workmen and sent, three east, three west, three north, three south and three in and about the temple, to search for the body."

"Where was it found?"

Ans. "Under a sprig of cassia, where a worthy brother sat down to rest and refresh himself."

"Was there anything particular took place on the discovery of the body?"

Ans. "There was, viz.: on moving the earth till we came to the coffin, we involuntarily found our hands in this position, to guard our nostrils against the offensive effluvia which arose from the grave."

"How long had the body lain there?"

Ans. "Fourteen days."

"What did they do with the body?"

Ans. "Raised it in a Masonic form and carried it up to the temple for more decent interment."

"Where was it buried?"

Ans. "Under the Sanctum Sanctorum, or holy of holies of King Solomon's Temple, over which they erected a marble monument, with this inscription delineated thereon: A virgin weeping over a broken column, with a book open before her, in her right hand a sprig of cassia, in her left an urn. Time standing behind her, with his hands infolded in the ringlets of her hair."

"What do they denote?"

Ans. "The weeping virgin denotes the unfinished state of the temple; the broken column, that one of the principal supports of Masonry had fallen; the book open before her, that his memory was on perpetual record; the sprig of cassia, the timely discovery of his grave; the urn in her left hand, that his ashes are safely deposited under the Sanctum Sanctorum, or holy of holies of King Solomon's Temple, and Time, standing behind her, with his hands infolded in the ringlets of her hair, that time, patience and perseverance will accomplish all things."

## SECTION SECOND.

"What does a Master's lodge represent?"

Ans. "The Sanctum Sanctorum, or holy of holies of King Solomon's Temple."

"How long was the temple building?"

Ans. Seven years, during which it rained not in the day-time, that the workmen might not be obstructed in their labor."

"What supported the temple."

Ans. "Fourteen hundred and fifty-three columns and two thousand nine hundred and six pilasters, all hewn from the finest Parian marble."

"What further supported it?"

Ans. "Three grand columns, or pillars."

"What were they called?"

Ans. "Wisdom, strength and beauty."

"What did they represent?"

Ans. "The pillar of wisdom represented Solomon, King of Israel, whose wisdom contrived the mighty fabric; the pillar of strength, Hiram, King of Tyre, who strengthened Solomon in his glorious undertaking; the pillar of beauty, Hiram Abiff, the widow's son, whose cunning craft and curious workmanship beautified and adorned the temple."

"How many were there employed in the building of King Solomon's Temple?"

Ans. "Three Grand Masters, three thousand three hundred Masters, or overseers of the work, eighty thousand Fellow Crafts, and seventy thousand Entered Apprentices; all those were classed and arranged in such a manner by the wisdom of Solomon that neither envy, discord nor confusion were suffered to interrupt that universal peace and tranquillity that pervaded the work at that important period."

"How many constitutes an Entered Apprentice lodge?"

Ans. "Seven; one Master and six Entered Apprentices."

"Where did they usually meet?"

Ans. "On the ground floor of King Solomon's Temple."

"How many constitute a Fellow Craft's lodge?"

Ans. "Five; two Masters and three Fellow Crafts."

"Where did they usually meet?"

Ans. "In the middle chamber of King Solomon's Temple."

"How many constitute a Master's lodge?"

Ans "Three Master Masons."

"Where did they usually meet?"

Ans. "In the Sanctum Sanctorum, or holy of holies of King Solomon's Temple."

"Have you any emblems on this degree?"

Ans. "We have several, which are divided into two classes."

"What are the first class?"

Ans. "The pot of incense, the bee-hive, the book of constitutions, guarded by the Tyler's sword, the sword pointing to a naked heart, the all-seeing eye, the anchor and ark, the forty-seventh problem of Euclid, the hour-glass, the scythe, and the three steps usually delineated on the Master's carpet, which are thus explained: The pot of incense is an emblem of a pure heart, which is always an acceptable sacrifice to the Deity and, as this glows with fervent heat, so should our hearts continually glow with gratitude to the great and beneficent Author of our existence for the manifold blessings and comforts we enjoy. The bee-hive is an emblem of industry, and recommends the practice of that virtue to all created beings, from the highest seraph in heaven to the lowest reptile of the dust. It teaches us that, as we came into the world rational and intelligent beings, so we should ever be industrious ones, never sitting down contented while our fellow-creatures around us are in want, when it is in our power to relieve them without inconvenience to ourselves. When we take a survey of nature, we behold man, in his infancy, more helpless and indigent than the brute creation; he lies languishing for days, weeks, months and years, totally incapable of providing sustenance for himself; of guarding against the attacks of the wild beasts of the field, or sheltering himself from the inclemencies of the weather. It might have pleased the great Creator of heaven and earth to have made man independent of all other beings, but, as dependence is one of the strongest bonds of society, mankind were made dependent on each other for protection and security, as they thereby enjoy better opportunities of fulfilling the duties of reciprocal love and friendship. Thus was man formed for social and active life, the noblest part of the work of God, and he that will so demean himself, as not to be endeavoring to add to the common stock of knowledge and understanding, may be deemed a drone in the hive of nature, a useless member of society, and unworthy of our protection as Masons.

The book of constitutions, guarded by the Tyler's sword, reminds us that we should be ever watchful and guarded in our thoughts, words, and actions, particularly when before the enemies of Masonry, ever bearing in remembrance those truly Masonic virtues, silence and circumspection. The sword pointing to a naked heart, demonstrates that justice will sooner or later overtake us; and although our thoughts, words and actions may be hidden from the eye of man yet that all-seeing eye, whom the sun, moon and stars obey, and under whose watchful care even comets perform their stupendous revolutions, pervades the inmost recesses of the human heart, and will reward us according to our merits. The anchor and ark, are emblems of a well grounded hope and a well spent life. They are emblematical of that Divine ark which safely wafts us over this tempestuous sea of troubles, and that anchor which shall safely moor us in a peaceful harbor, where the wicked cease from troubling, and the weary shall find rest.

The forty-seventh problem of Euclid: This was an invention of our ancient friend and brother, the great Pythagoras, who, in his travels through Asia, Africa and Europe, was initiated into several orders of priesthood, and raised to the sublime degree of a Master Mason. This wise philosopher enriched his mind abundantly in a general knowledge of things, and more especially in Geometry, or Masonry, on this subject he drew out many problems and theorems; and among the most distinguished he erected this, which, in the joy of his heart, he called Eureka, in the Grecian language signifying, I have found it; and upon the discovery of which he is said to have sacrificed a hecatomb. It teaches Masons to be general lovers of the arts and sciences. The hour glass is an emblem of human life. Behold! how swiftly the sands run, and how rapidly our lives are drawing to a close. We cannot without astonishment behold the little particles which are contained in this machine; how they pass away, almost imperceptibly, and yet to our surprise in a short space of an hour they are all exhausted. Thus wastes man! To-day, he puts forth the tender leaves of hope; to-morrow, blossoms, and bears his blushing honors thick upon him; the next day comes a frost, which nips the root, and when he thinks his greatness is still ripening, he falls like autumn leaves, to enrich our mother earth. The scythe is an emblem of time, which cuts the brittle thread of life, and launches us into eternity. Behold! what havoc the scythe of time makes among the human race; if by chance we should escape the numerous evils, incident to childhood and youth, and with health and vigor come to the years of manhood, yet withal we must soon be cut down by the all-devouring scythe of time, and be gathered into the land where our fathers have gone before us. The three steps usually delineated upon the Masters carpet, are emblematical of the three principal stages of human life, viz.: youth, manhood and age. In youth, as Entered Apprentices, we ought industriously to occupy our minds in the attainment of useful knowledge; in manhood, as Fellow Craft, we should apply our knowledge to the discharge of our respective duties to God, our neighbors, and ourselves, that so in age, as Master Mason, we may enjoy the happy reflections consequent on a well spent life, and die in the hope of a glorious immortality.

"What are the second class of emblems?"

Ans. "The spade, coffin, death-head, marrow-bones; and sprig of cassia, which are thus explained: The spade opens the vault to receive our bodies where our active limbs will soon moulder to dust. The coffin, death-head, and marrow-bones, are emblematical of the death and burial, of our Grand Master, Hiram Abiff, and are worthy of our serious attention. The sprig of cassia is emblematical of that important part of man which never dies—and when the cold winter of death shall have passed, and the bright summer's morn of the resurrection appears, the Son of Righteousness shall descend, and send forth his angels to collect our ransomed dust; then, if we are found worthy, by his pass word, we shall enter into the celestial lodge above, where the Supreme Architect of the Universe presides, where we shall see the King in the beauty of holiness and with him enter into an endless eternity. Here ends the three first degrees of Masonry, which constitute a Master Mason's Lodge. A Master Mason's Lodge and a chapter of Royal Arch Masons, are two distinct bodies, wholly independent of each other. The members of a Chapter are privileged to visit all Master Mason's Lodges when they please, and may be, and often are members of both at the same time; and all the members of a Master Mason's Lodge, who are Royal Arch Masons, though not members of any Chapter, may visit any Chapter. I wish the reader to understand that neither all Royal Arch Masons nor Master Masons are members of either Lodge or Chapter; there are tens of thousands who are not members and scarcely ever attend, although privileged to do so. A very small proportion of Masons, comparatively speaking, ever advance any further than the third degree, and consequently never get the great word which was lost by Hiram's untimely death. Solomon, king of Israel; Hiram, king of Tyre, and Hiram Abiff; the widow's son having sworn that they nor neither of them would ever give the word except they three were present; [and it is generally believed that there was not another person in the world at that time that had it], consequently the word was lost, and supposed to be forever; but the sequel will show it was found after the lapse of four hundred and seventy years; notwithstanding the word Mah-hah-bone, which was substituted by Solomon, still continues to be used by Master Masons, and no doubt will be as long as Masonry attracts the attention of men; and the word which was lost is used in the Royal Arch degree.

What was the word of the Royal Arch degree before they found the Master's word which was lost at the death of Hiram Abiff, and was not found for four hundred and seventy years? Were there any Royal Arch Masons before the Master's word was found? I wish some Masonic gentleman would solve these two questions. The ceremonies, history, and the lecture, in the preceding degree, are so similar, that perhaps, some one of the three might have been dispensed with, and the subject well understood by most readers, notwithstanding, there is a small difference between the work and history, and between the history and the lecture. I shall now proceed with the Mark Master's degree, which is the first degree in the Chapter. The Mark Master's degree, the Past Master's, and the Most Excellent Master's are called lodges of Mark Master Masons, Past Masters, and Most Excellent Masters; yet, although called lodges, they are a component part of the Chapter. Ask a Mark Master Mason if he belongs to the Chapter, he will tell you he does, but that he has only been marked. It is not an uncommon thing, by any means, for a Chapter to confer all four of the degrees in one night, viz.: The Mark Master, Past Master, Most Excellent Master, and Royal Arch degree.

# FREEMASONRY AT A GLANCE.

## ENTERED APPRENTICE DEGREE.

The Holy Bible on the altar is usually opened at the 123d Psalm and the square and compass placed thereon, the latter open and both points placed below the square.

PREPARATION OF CANDIDATE ENTERED APPRENTICE DEGREE.—He is ushered into the "*preparation* room," where he meets the Junior Deacon and Stewards who divest him of all his clothing except his shirt. He is then handed an old pair of drawers which he puts on; the left leg is rolled up above the knee; the left sleeve of the shirt is rolled up above the elbow, a hoodwink is fastened over both eyes, a rope, called a cable-tow, is put once around his neck, and a slipper (with the heel slip-shod) is put upon the *right* foot.

Preparation in Entered Apprentice Degree.

Penal Sign.    Due Guard.

DUE GUARD OF AN ENTERED APPRENTICE—Hold out the left hand a little in front of the body and in a line with the lower button of the vest, the hand being open and palm turned upward. Now place the right hand horizontally across the left and about two or three inches above it.

PENAL SIGN OF AN ENTERED APPRENTICE.—Made from the due-guard by dropping the left hand carelessly; at the same time raise the right arm and draw the hand, still open, across the throat, thumb next the throat, and drop the hand perpendicularly by the side. These movements ought to be made in an off hand manner, without stiffness.

SIGN WITHOUT DUE-GUARDS—(The usual way outside the lodge.) Simply draw the open hand carelessly across the throat and let it fall down by the side.

Candidate taking Entered Apprentice Obligation.

Worshipful Master to Candidate:—"You will advance to the altar, kneel upon your naked left knee, your right forming a square, your left hand supporting the holy Bible, square and compass, your right resting thereon, in which due form you will say, I, with your name in full, and repeat after me."

GRIP OF AN ENTERED APPRENTICE.—Take hold of each other's hands as in ordinary hand-shaking and press the top of your thumb hard against the first knuckle-joint of the first finger near the hand. If the person whom you are shaking hands with is a Mason, he will generally return a like pressure on your hand.

ENTERED APPRENTICE WORD—Boaz. It is the name of this grip.

ENTERED APPRENTICE STEP.—Step off one step with the left foot and bring the heel of your right foot to the hollow of your left.

The Holy Bible ought to be opened at the 7th chapter of Amos and one point of the compass elevated above the square.

PREPARATION OF CANDIDATE FELLOW CRAFT DEGREE.—He is ushered into the "preparation room" as before, and divested of all his clothing as in the preceding degree. In this case the *right* leg of the old drawers is raised up above the knee, the *right* sleeve of the shirt is rolled up above the elbow, the slipper is now put upon the *left* foot, the *left* heel being slip shod. The hoodwink is again put over both eyes and the cable-tow is put twice around the naked *right arm* and an apron tied on, in which condition he is "duly and truly prepared" and led by the Junior Deacon to the door of the lodge as before.

Dress of Fellow Craft.

Worshipful Master to Candidate:—You will advance to the altar, kneel upon your naked right knee, your left forming a square, your right hand resting on the Holy Bible, square and compass, your left forming a right angle supported by the square in which due form you will say, "I," with your name in full, and repeat after me.

Candidate taking Fellow Craft Obligation. [The left arm should be perpendicular.]

DUE GUARD OF A FELLOW CRAFT.—Hold out the right hand a little from the body and on a line with the lower button of the vest, the palm being open and turned down-ward; also raise the left arm so as to form a right angle at the elbow, from the shoulder to the elbow being horizontal and fore-arm perpendicular.

SIGN OF A FELLOW CRAFT.—Made from the due-guard by dropping the left hand carelessly to the side and at the same time raise the right hand to the left breast, with the palm towards the breast and the fingers a little crooked; then draw the hand smartly across the breast from left to right and let it drop perpendicularly to the side.

Due Guard.

Sign Fellow Craft

SIGN WITHOUT DUE GUARD.—The usual way out side the lodge). Draw the right hand, palm open and fingers a little crooked, smartly across the breast from left to right and drop it carelessly by your side.

PASS GRIP OF A FELLOW CRAFT.—Take each other's hands as in ordinary hand-shaking and press the top of your thumb hard against the space between the first and second knuckles of the right hand. Should the person whose hand you hold be a Fellow Craft, he will return a like pressure on your hand, or else may give you the grip of an Entered Apprentice.

PASS OF FELLOW CRAFT—Shibboleth. It is the name of this grip.

REAL GRIP OF A FELLOW CRAFT.—Take each other by the right hand as in ordinary hand-shaking and press top of your thumb hard against the second knuckle. Should the man whose hand you shake be a Fellow Craft, he will return a similar pressure on your hand, or may possibly give you any one of the two preceding grips.

WORD OF FELLOW CRAFT—Jachin. It is the name of this the *real grip.*

FELLOW CRAFT OR SECOND STEP.—Step off one step with the right foot and bring the heel of the left foot to the hollow of the right; your feet forming the angle of an oblong square.

## MASTER MASON'S DEGREE.

The Holy Bible ought to be opened at the 12th chapter of Ecclesiastes and both points of the compass elevated above the square.

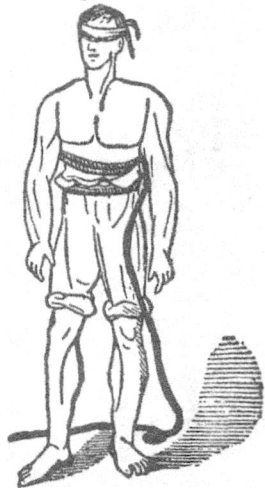

PREPARATION OF CANDIDATE MASTER MASON'S DEGREE.—He is conducted into the preparation room as in the preceding degree. All his clothing is removed as before; both legs of the drawers are tucked up above the knees, both sleeves of the shirt are tucked up above the elbows, both breasts of the shirt are turned, making both breasts bare. The hoodwink is again fastened over both eyes and the cable-tow is put three times around his body. No slipper is used in this degree. Should the shirt be closed in front, it must be taken off or turned front backwards, as both breasts must be bare. An apron is then tied on and worn as a Fellow Craft, and thus he is "duly and truly prepared."

Preparation of Candidate in Master Masons Degree.

**Candidate taking Master Mason's Obligation.**

Worshipful Master to Candidate, "You will advance to the altar, kneel upon both your naked knees, both hands resting n the Holy Bible, square and compass in which due form you will say, "I," with your name in full and repeat after me"

DUE-GUARD OF A MASTER MASON.—Extend both hands in front of the body on a line with the lower button of the vest with the palms open and turned downward, both hands being close together, thumbs nearly touching.

SIGN OF A MASTER MASON.—Made from the due-guard by dropping the left hand carelessly and drawing the right across the body from left to right side on a line with the lower button of the vest, the hand being open as before, palm downward and the thumb towards the body.

Due-guard Penal Sign, Then drop the hand perpendicularly to
Master   Master Ma-   the side.
Mason.   son.

SIGN WITHOUT DUE-GUARD.—(Ordinary manner outside the lodge.) Simply draw the right hand as above described, carelessly across the body and drop it by the side.

PASS-GRIP OF A MASTER MASON —Take hold of each other's hands as in ordinary hand shaking and press the top of your thumb hard against the space between the second and third knuckles. Should the man whose hand you shake be a Mason he may return or give any previous grip.

PASS OF MASTER MASON—Tubal Cain. It is the name of this grip.

STRONG GRIP OF A MASTER MASON OR LION'S PAW.—Grasp each other's right hands very firmly, the spaces between the thumb and first finger being interlocked and the tops of the fingers being pressed hard against each other's wrist where it joins the hand, the fingers of each being somewhat spread.

CANDIDATE AS HIRAM ABIFF FALLING INTO THE CANVAS, having been struck in the forehead by the setting maul of the supposed third ruffian, Jubelum.

FIVE POINTS OF FELLOWSHIP.

Five Points of Fellowship.

Worshipful Master:—Which are the five points of fellowship?

Senior Deacon:—Foot to foot (Master and candidate extend their right feet, placing the inside of one against that of the other). Knee to knee (they bring their right knees together); breast to breast (they bring their right breasts together); hand to back (Master places his left hand on the candidate's back, the candidate's is placed by the Deacon on the Master's back); cheek to cheek or mouth to ear (Master puts his mouth to candidate's right ear thus bringing the right cheek of each together. See figure).

MASTER'S WORDS—(whispered in the ear of the candidate), *Mah-hah bone*, after which the candidate whispers the same word in the Master's ear.